THE POOREST MAN IN ZION

THE POOREST MAN IN ZION

WEALTH BEYOND THE RICHES OF BABYLON

DAVID BENSON

FIRST EDITION FIRST PRINTING

Published by David Benson Coaching
North Logan, Utah. See www.DavidBenson.us for full contact information.

Copyright © 2019 by David Benson
All rights reserved. Neither this book nor any part thereof may be used, reproduced, transmitted, distributed, or stored in any manner or format whatever without prior written permission of the author, except in the case of brief quotations embodied in critical articles or reviews.

Liability and Warranty Disclaimer. While every effort has been made to ensure informational accuracy in this book, the author and publisher do not assume and hereby disclaim any liability for loss, damage, or disruption caused by omissions, errors, or content use of any type whatsoever. No explicit nor implied warranty or guarantee is extended. Narrative elements in this work spawn from the author's experience, study, and imagination and are used in a fictitious manner.

Book design by David Benson. Frontispiece, *Zion: City of Light*, by Emily Benson.

Printed in the United States of America
First Edition First Printing | March 01, 2019 (version 2019.03.7)
10 9 8 7 6 5 4 3 2 1

LCCN: 2019902188
ISBN-13: 978-1-7337711-0-8 (eBook)
ISBN-13: 978-1-7337711-1-5 (paperback)
ISBN-13: 978-1-7337711-2-2 (hardcover)
BISAC Subject Headings:
    BUS107000 BUSINESS & ECONOMICS / Personal Success
    POL05100 POLITICAL SCIENCE / Utopias
    REL046000 RELIGION / Christianity /
        Church of Jesus Christ of Latter-day Saints (Mormon)
    SEL016000 SELF-HELP / Personal Growth / Happiness

If you purchased this book without a cover, be aware that this book is stolen property. It was reported as "unsold and destroyed" to the publisher, and neither the author nor the publisher has received any payment for this "stripped" book.

Please visit www.DavidBenson.us for background and offering information.

To Stacy, my Stacy

~ ~ ~

I am forever grateful for divine direction, for human patience, and for personal persistence.

"Long ago in a promised land prospered a people pure in heart, unfettered from malice. Fled but not forgotten, Zion awaits revival."
—David Benson

"It is safe to tell the pure in heart that they shall see God, for only the pure in heart want to."
—C. S. Lewis

Contents

Foreword ix

Introduction xiii

  1. The Man Who Desired Happiness 1

  2. Free to Choose 22

  3. One Heart and One Mind 42

  4. Dwelt in Righteousness 62

  5. The Laborer Is Worthy of His Hire 82

  6. All Things in Common 105

  7. No Poor Among Them 124

  8. Lie Down in Safety 141

  9. No More Strangers 159

10. Teach All Nations 171

An Historical Sketch of Zion 185

The Author and His Book 194

Foreword

WHAT DO WE CRAVE? WHAT will we unfailingly seek when it is lacking, though never tire of once it is gained? What will satiate our most profound human desires, yet remain pristine and vibrant?

Our universal, mortal experience supplies us with ample settings to crave things, from the most basic necessities of life to the most complicated emotional needs of societal interaction. It seems that we are continually lacking one thing or another and ever struggling to grasp that elusive want. Living in a world bursting with variety amid uniformity—unique opportunities strewn across similar circumstances—surely we can uncover *some* pursuit that will once and forever heal our lives of cyclical emptiness. What is it that will completely fill the desperate void and still leave room for more?

In 1926, George Samuel Clason, an American map-maker and publisher, attempted to answer this timeless question in a volume entitled *The Richest Man in Babylon*. In the foreword to that now celebrated work, Clason declared that what we all desire is a reliable stream of income, invulnerable to the ups and downs of future economies. Through ten separate essays, he drew upon common knowledge and personal experience to explain how to secure and retain monetary affluence, recounting general principles and simple examples to support the quest for great riches. That financial advice took the form of parables set around the ancient city of Babylon, a place of wealth and wonder, with characters succeeding or failing in their commercial efforts as they heeded or abandoned the described doctrines. A residual fortune, Clason claimed, was the means to gaining pleasure, stability, notoriety, conquest—anything we wanted now and everything we might crave later. Money was happiness. Riches were what we all should seek.

I disagree. I seek something more. We *all* seek something more.

When we are true to ourselves, when we are able to step back from the distracting chaos and blinding cacophony of our everyday existence, we admit in our hearts to an authentic yearning for that which will uplift us. Is it the pecuniary opulence that money represents? No. Is it non-stop entertainment, carnal gratification, cursory power, or superficial fame? Again, no. These and similar objects are the candy of life, the refined sugar and empty calories that tempt the eye and please the tongue, but result in rotten teeth, disrupted bowels, and malnourished bodies. They deliver only fleeting pleasures that feed our cravings for a moment, then leave us as hungry as ever.

Instead, we seek that which silver and gold cannot purchase. We seek that which is more sustaining, more wholesome, more meaty—a savory something that will nourish. We yearn for love and belonging, kindness and understanding, harmonious relationships, noble initiatives, robust enterprises, transcendence. These are the whole fruits and vegetables of healthy living, the natural grains, the lean meats and fishes, the healing herbs and tasty spices—the pulse of life. They feed our souls, nurturing within us genuine success, flourishing reality, and that which we all ultimately desire: lasting happiness.

The Poorest Man in Zion is a response to Clason's classic compilation. It purposefully mimics, albeit loosely, the format and tenor of his original foreword—more properly a preface—and of his original ten parables, of the author's brief biography, and of the informal introduction and brief historical sketch that were added to subsequent editions. I am grateful to have had the chance to digest and appreciate his writings. We are indebted to those who have gone before us, on whose shoulders we stand to make our own contributions.

Through a series of ten comparable essays, *The Poorest Man in Zion* reviews the principles that lead to living life to its fullest, to overcoming the sadness and pitfalls of human experience, and to becoming perpetually happy as individuals and communities. This work relies on cohesive parables—examined independently or as a progressive story—from the days of venerable Zion, the City of Holiness, featuring characters who explore and expound upon its philosophies. The concluding article, "An Historical Sketch of Zion," provides helpful context for the tales, and will prove most useful when studied as a prelude to the essays. A related but separate volume is planned for future publication under the title *A Practical Zion: The Companion Guide to The Poorest Man in Zion*, and expects to serve as a pragmatic blueprint for implementing the described behavioral principles in a contemporary setting.

Zion was the land where the people of God dwelt in peace and freedom for hundreds of years. They lived apart from, while surrounded by, the wickedness of neighboring societies that would gradually result in the flood of Noah and eventually give rise to the famed city of Babylon. While striving to become pure in their own hearts, the citizens of Zion graciously entwined themselves with the inhabitants of adjacent lands—lands from whence they themselves had migrated. Their constant hope was to share the benefits of their culture and to welcome into their company as many as would accept it.

While *The Poorest Man in Zion* endeavors to stylistically follow Clason's masterwork, it charts a decidedly different course in purpose and content. Zion is the antithesis of Babylon, exemplifying the pure love of God as opposed to the love of money, contrasting uplifting joy with debilitating despair. In mortality, we live on a continuum between the two states, unable to fully embrace the one until we elect to fully cast off the other. Happiness is the overarching goal of our worldly sojourn and will be its consequence, if only we resolve to pursue the principles that lead to it. If individual and, by extension, national prosperity *indeed* depend upon financial riches, then perhaps Babylon would be a fit model to mirror. However, if personal and collective thriving *instead* depend upon lasting happiness, then Zion must be our aim.

—David Benson, Author

THE POOREST MAN IN ZION IS WEALTHY BEYOND THE RICHEST MAN IN BABYLON

Introduction

BEHIND EACH OF US, STRETCHING back through the past like a potholed road, lies the ruin of bad judgement, the sadness inherent in poor choices. Mistakes great and small, regrets hot and cold, offenses, fears, and doubts all fade from sight in our rearview mirror. Whether the traveled distance is short or long, none of us may avoid the challenges and stumblings of human existence. Some see wide holes, deep and many. Others see mere pockmarks, shallow and few. Every broken road extracts its distinctive, sorrowful toll.

Ahead of us, stretching into the future through tinted glass, rolls the road not yet taken, lying fresh and level, shimmering with hope for a smoother ride. Along *this* highway appear the unmade decisions that will determine how we fill our remaining miles, the stations storing fuel that will drive us forward, and the signposts that will steer our most earnest efforts. The manner of our travel will govern the landmarks we expect to experience and the garage where we finally park when our tanks run dry. We are cruising carriages, crowded with potential bliss.

For us to be successful in life, our purpose must extend beyond the vain attempt to survive it. We must learn to thrive, regardless of our circumstances. We must transcend. Let us profit from the enduring behavioral principles recounted in the pages that follow. Allow them to lead us away from the sterility of passing pleasure and towards the fruitfulness of lasting happiness. Like the laws of motion, they are as manifest as they are practical. May they prove for us, as they have proven for others, a steadfast means to personal progress, and a reliable route to discovering joy.

LO, HAPPINESS IS ABIDING FOR THOSE WHO APPRECIATE THE BASIC LAWS OF ITS ATTAINMENT

1. HAPPINESS IS OUR DEEPEST DESIRE
2. FREEDOM EMPOWERS CHOICE
3. MUTUAL VISION UNITES PEOPLE
4. PROMISING GOALS DRIVE ACTION
5. MIGHTY LABOR YIELDS ABUNDANCE
6. SURPLUS CREATES SHARED SAVINGS
7. PRUDENT WELFARE ENRICHES ALL
8. PREPARATION PROMOTES SECURITY
9. ADVOCATES WELCOME THE ASPIRING
10. OUTREACH EXPANDS INFLUENCE

I

THE MAN WHO DESIRED HAPPINESS

JUBAL WAS EXHAUSTED. THE ONCE-POPULAR musician of Haner exhaled deeply as he lowered his distinctive flute from his lips to his lap, then set it aside to rest atop the low, stone wall upon which he sat. The desert sun beat upon his limp but muscular frame. His indifferent hand flopped aimlessly at his side, raising a cloud of dust that would slowly settle, unnoticed, back onto his thigh. Hanging above the dreary street, his lower legs dangled haphazardly, not long enough to reach the sandy grains below, not interested enough to make the effort. Another day had dawned, another week had begun, but he barely noticed their passing. It mattered little to the musician. It mattered not at all.

Despite his appearance, it was not Jubal's body that was weary, still strong and vibrant with barely thirty-eight years of life. Neither was it his mind that needed repose, for his thoughts and reasoning were as sharp as the fine copper knife that had fashioned his now-famous flute of nine pipes. No, notwithstanding the unrelenting attacks of hardship and torment he had suffered over the course of these last years, his mind and body were both healthy and sound. It was his *soul* that was drained, worn-out from the thudding sorrow that had crashed against his once-happy humanity. It had beaten down his will to continue and, like the black drums of recent war, its echoes still tormented him day and night. It was his *heart* that was exhausted.

Practically bent in half, Jubal reached down and lifted his instrument once more from the stubborn wall, only raising it as far as his chin before giving up and returning it to the dusty ledge. He had sat slouched on his miserable perch for nearly two hours, but had not been able to bring himself to play any music. His curly, unkempt hair—still radiant red beneath layers of grime—fell into his empty, brown eyes. His bare head bowed as his hands collapsed back into his lap, this time not bothering to replace his instrument on its shelf.

He looked at his fingers, stiff and cracked from excessive contact with the elements. He remembered how they used to be quick and nimble, back when he would play his flute for the pleasure of his listeners and for the welcome gift of their gold. His sole garment, a torn and pale cloak of fine workmanship, had been purchased with those bygone riches. Now, its sturdy threads were ripped and its vibrant colors were faded, as were his hopes for returning to the good life he had lost. He wondered if that life had ever been as good as he remembered.

"Ho there young lad," called a deep voice, gentle with age and sorrow of its own. "Could this ghost sitting before me in the morning sunlight possibly be my friend Jubal? Your uncovered head looks to be his, but I cannot see your face to be sure, my eyes as dim as they are in my long years. You must play me a tune so I can discern your true identity. Deceivers are all too common in our streets these days, but none can match my friend's skill on his flute of nine pipes. By your music, I will know if you are truly him."

"Good morning, Mahijah," Jubal whispered, his parched throat finding no energy to equal even the puny attempt at enthusiasm from this passerby. "What brings you past my crumbling wall this wretched day?"

Jubal forced a reply without raising his eyes, recognizing the old man's voice as that of the temperate optimist who had become, within only the last five months, a reliable friend. With his head still lowered, Jubal could just make out the long, thin legs and swollen feet of the shepherd of Sharon who had recently taken up residence outside the southern walls of his new city in a small, rocky house with thatched roof. His sandals were covered in the distinctive, dried droppings of the small flock of sheep he tended there and which, like the house, he had claimed for himself, they both having been abandoned by their previous owners.

"*Good morning?*" Mahijah countered with feigned surprise. "Why, the day cannot be as gloomy as you claim if you have the heart to wish me good in it. As usual, I come to trade in the market with our fellow sojourners round the land of Haner. I carry with me the scant spun cloth and the limited sewn cloaks that remain in my inventory. Before they start to decay, I need to convert them into a set of copper shears, or at least into copper coins for my empty purse. I have not seen you on the wall for at least a week. I feared that you had given up on your music entirely."

"I well-nigh did, and may yet still," the musician complained to his one and only friend, the sole person who would listen to him. "I have only played to myself, sitting in the dirt next to the ruins of my father's dwelling, and not more than three times since we last met. Today is the second day in seven I have tried to play in public, but again could not manage it. Yesterday, I could barely lift myself to sit on this rocky hedge, and then not even to pull myself erect. I suppose being here at all is progress."

"Yes, indeed it is. I am pleased to see you once more. Will you play a melody for me before I enter the square—some luck to speed shekels into my lonely sack?" asked Mahijah, patting the worn and grayed cloak at his hip, presumably where a slim stash of currency was securely fastened. But his tapping was the only indication of a purse at all, for no bulge could be seen beneath his robes, and not even the tinkling of two measly coins could be heard.

Jubal could not stop a tiny, involuntary smile from forming at his lips, but he made an effort to hide it from his friend. He had become so attached to the plentiful pain his past had supplied that he was loathe to let it go completely, though he reluctantly recognized the earliest hints of it starting to fade. He raised the pan flute to his lips and mustered a doleful tune from the instrument. The liveliness he had usually felt when playing a song welled up inside him, and he started to remember more cheerful days. But after just a few dozen notes, he stopped short and lowered the pipes, succumbing to overwhelming gloom once more.

"So mournful, Jubal," Mahijah sighed with his eyes closed, shaking his gray head back and forth. "And yet, so beautiful. My ears can understand why you were once the most preferred musical artist in all of the city. Those remaining few who buy cloth and cloak from me still speak of your skill with your custom-made flute. Your fame throughout Haner persists, and they are sad that you have not played in so long. I only wish I could have heard your songs back when you piped for huge crowds, moving them to sing and dance in the lanes and the marketplace, forgetting their troubles for a moment to bask in the splendor of your music. That must have been a sight to see! My weak heart thrills whenever I think of it. Is it likely that something more than tears over past agonies has led you to give it up? Perhaps you have lost your gift from the gods."

"Gift? *Gods*?" Jubal cried in disbelief, abruptly finding his voice and startling the old herdsman so much that he almost fell backwards, nearly dropping the last of the cloaks he had managed to sew from his meager harvest of wool. Jubal himself was shocked by the venom that flew from his lips, and his mood instantly softened.

"Gift?" he offered tenderly in self-reproval, realizing the dread he must have caused the shepherd. Jubal tightly grasped his pan flute between strong fingers, slowly shaking it for emphasis. "No, this is no gift, but skill hard-earned through relentless practice. I have labored long and with great effort to train these fingers—these lips—to produce music praised by all who hear it. It is what earned me silver and gold to fill many chests. Nor did the gods make my struggles any easier. A hundred times *no*. It was my sweat and sleepless nights that created the music you hear flowing from my flute. The love of my parents and of my dear wife: those were gifts, gifts lost forever. There was no mercy from the gods to save any of them from the outrages of war. But you know my story as well as I. Please, let us not slog through the muck and the mire of those woeful tales. I do not have the heart to tell them again."

With this the musician leaned forward, retaining his flute in the one hand while stretching out the other and resting it on his friend's shoulder, using it to cushion his small hop down from the wall. He drew close so that the herdsman could more easily see him. Jubal was done with music for the day, but maybe tomorrow or a more distant dawn when he could summon the strength, he would try again. With a smirk of frank reflection, he admitted to himself that his intentions were insincere—that he was unlikely to make another attempt. At least he could be honest.

Meanwhile, Mahijah gathered himself from the jolt of Jubal's outburst and found his friend's taut face with his hand, offering his thoughtful and conciliatory reply. "You are right, my dear artist. I have no doubt your craft is one earned after years of personal exertion and sacrifice. I meant no insult. And your history of sorrow, I know it well, as well as you know mine."

Jubal closed his eyes, trance-like, forcing himself to remember. From a young age, he had learned to play the pan flute of many pipes, an instrument his father had fashioned while relaxing between constructing the carpentry items he sold to provide a living for his small family: his wife, his son, and two daughters. When Jubal was not completing chores or helping his father build a piece of furniture, he relished dancing about their small house, which was situated against the outer southern wall within the mighty fortifications of Haner. He would blow on his beloved flute as he blissfully swayed to the music, his mother smiling and cheering, his baby sisters twirling in circles and squealing with delight.

It was a happy childhood. His mother taught him to care for his younger siblings and to develop a gentle demeanor. His father trained him to work hard and to be honest with friends and strangers alike. They both encouraged him to develop his musical talents, as long as they did not interfere with his household responsibilities. The developing artist loved skipping without a care through the dusty streets on the outskirts of the city's center, making music to gratify his heart and to delight the friends, neighbors, and strangers he met along the way.

As Jubal grew in stature and knowledge, his skill at the flute blossomed. He quickly found that he could earn extra money for his parents by sitting in the gates of the city playing for travelers and traders as they passed by. Though grateful for his contribution, his parents preferred that he help with his father's woodwork and develop carpentry as his formal trade. They scolded him often for avoiding those duties, but he held no passion for working with timber. He continued to sneak away from the house each day to find a place to play his songs.

The maturing musician soon became so good at his hobby that wealthy families of the city would seek him out to play at weddings and at parties, for audiences small and large. As rapidly as his talent grew, so did the contents of his purse. Unfortunately, so too grew his indignant pride, and his impatience with his mother and father. As he approached the age of independence from his parents, he became more and more vicious towards them and increasingly angry at their demands. Following a particularly violent argument in the workshop, he forsook his father's trade and stormed from his childhood dwelling, committed to pursue his music and to find a residence of his own. He then rushed headlong into marriage with a young, native woman named Hannah whom he had known from adolescence, but for whom he felt only the beginnings of true love.

Taking the wealth that Jubal had previously accumulated, the couple immediately purchased a grandiose house and began spending his silver and gold on a lavish standard of living. Uninhibited parties, unwise purchases, and scarce self-restraint became routine, wasting any surplus they may have once owned. The husband and wife became enthralled with empty praise from false friends who were intent on taking advantage of any generosity they could pull from the couple. Soon, they were spending more time with their money and with impostors than they were with each other, and Jubal's fame only served to aggravate the problem. Envy and suspicion crept into their relationship, magnified by insecurities characteristic of keeping up appearances. Their love withered.

Sadness became commonplace in their household. Although the couple had been loyal friends as older youth, the selfishness demonstrated by their lifestyle led to the inevitable souring of their marriage. Jubal spent his days out of their house and away from her, applying his art towards increasingly frantic commitments to deliver performances. Hannah spent her days alone with resentment and gossiping neighbors, unable to bear any children to give her solace. Granted that the partners had possessed plenty of resources at the start of their joint life, their outlays simply could not keep pace with their earnings, and any savings stored against calamity were steadily depleted.

Despite the remnants of sincere love for his spouse, things only worsened for the young man. He focused his energies on regaining his fortune, thinking that more gold would resolve the conflicts with his wife, and hoping that they might renew their dedication towards each other. Towards that end, he did enjoy some initial success. But with the temporary return of riches came the reoccurrence of sadness, the betrayal of untrue companions, the constant danger of theft, and the insidious comparing and coveting of riches. Conspiring voices—whispers in back passages— were always threatening to take away for naught what he had built with his energy and dedication. It appeared as if nothing could be done to reverse the course of their distressed lives.

Then, greater tragedy struck. Although the walls of Haner were a formidable defense, war with nearby kingdoms was common in the region, and its ravages ever just one angry noble away from the city doors. One inevitable day, messengers rushed through Haner's avenues clamoring that an army of Heni was invading the land. Jubal's fame by this time had grown so grand that he earned the notice of the king. He was called away from his wife and residence to the inner keep of his lord, to soothe him with music during preparations for war. But the army of Heni was too swift for Haner's forces to make ready a defense. Before adequate resources could be placed in store, the enemy handily cut the city off from its farmlands and laid siege to its occupants. Jubal was forced to stand by the king in his innermost fortifications, forbidden to return to his wife or failing riches.

By the fortieth day of the siege, a tenth of the city had starved and another tenth had fallen prey to disease. Heni's army eventually crashed through a portion of the southern outer wall, pillaging the inhabitants in brutal fashion and forcing the war-weary residents and their defenders to take flight. With Haner's forces in panicky retreat, and with their broken king at the head of the evacuation, Jubal could no longer be kept against his will. He used his tenuous freedom to run to his house in a desperate search for Hannah, only to learn from neighbors that she had been carried away by the invaders, apparently lost forever. His heart broke, but there was no time to grieve properly. Hastening to his parent's residence, he hoped to find at least *some* of his family alive. Instead, he found the house covered with rocky debris from the broken wall, felled by the war machines of the enemy, with his parents and sisters crushed inside. His heart broke again, and he sank to the ground in tears.

The entire city was lost. Jubal's only choice was to flee for his life as the terrors of war raged about him, but he was captured like the majority of his remaining neighbors. Heni's victory was complete, but the enemy did not wish to occupy the city for itself. Rather, it desired a perpetual source of tribute from the survivors who were allowed to return to their city—with a severe condition. They were forced to pledge a fifth of their possessions in perpetuity to the king of Heni, a grievous burden to be sure. With no relief from despair forthcoming, Jubal's broken heart turned cold.

That was two years ago, and since then Haner's subjugated people had mostly returned to their city to rebuild, a gradual process due to the overwhelming taxes imposed upon them. While the population slowly increased, it was to never fully be replenished, and the spirit within the city turned noticeably more somber and discouraging than before the attack. Jubal's heart refused to mend. He gave up on being happy. He abandoned his music, declining to perform any other work. As a consequence, he was reduced to begging in the byways and avenues, which was where Mahijah first encountered him.

"Come, join me in the square," requested the old man, not surrendering to the artist's obvious melancholy. "I could use a strong arm to carry my load, and a comforting voice to remind me of happier times."

Jubal started from his reverie. Today was the first day of the week, a designated trading day at the marketplace for the occupants of Haner. Despite the city being devastated by the most recent war, market days were becoming more and more hectic, packed with shoppers. Mahijah did not do well in crowds, so a helping hand was most welcome.

Jubal took his friend's bundle of cloaks and cloth from him, laid it on his own shoulder, and began to walk with him towards the center of the city. The musician admired the cloak maker's expert work out loud. "I see that you are still able to spin cloth into fine garments. They remind me of the clothes I used to wear when I was a wealthy man, though they are not as brazen. Your colors are more subdued, more elegant. I imagine it took you many years to master your dexterity with a needle."

Mahijah reflected on the events that had brought him to this day. He was the son of a shepherd of Sharon, the land of green pastures and plentiful streams. The youngest of seven children, his mother died giving him birth, and his father and older siblings unfairly held him responsible for her passing, emotionally shunning and physically bruising him. His childhood was full of the hard work and suffering so common to most people of the time. Toil never seemed to end, and food never seemed sufficient. Not only did he tend the flocks near his lowly village with his brothers, but out of necessity, he also labored alongside his lone sister to perform the chores of the house: fetching water, mending clothes, cooking meals, refreshing bedding, and a whole host of related chores. Regardless of his hardships, he still found snippets of joy as he could, playing among the sheep, swimming in a nearby pond, or decorating the house with small patches of colorful cloth that he spun and stained himself.

Mahijah grew to be a fine shepherd and cloak maker despite his situation. The threat of warfare was as common to him as it would later be to Jubal, though his family was more subject to the robbery and abuse of raiders since they lived further from the walls and soldiers of their governing city. His family was also subject to the horrors of famine and drought, relying on the gods to favor them with good weather for grass, and on good grass for its flocks. As he approached the age of marriage, his father and three eldest brothers died in a famine. The eldest surviving brother took the house for his own, forcing Mahijah and his remaining siblings to fend for themselves. His brother and sister found shelter as servants in a larger household, the generosity of which was not to be extended to a third, hungry mouth.

He did find swift mercy from an older couple, who gave him a place to live and rescued him from hunger. Their only child, much older than Mahijah, was a smiling, joyful girl who had moved away a few years earlier. She was constantly traveling to and fro in the land, returning at unexpected times after being away for months on end. She was always eager to share the details of her journeys with her parents, though they preferred to spend their mutual moments chiding her for not finding a husband, and for abandoning them to growing old alone. Mahijah could grasp little of their conversations, but he did remember hearing her speak of a special land where nobody hungered nor thirsted and where everyone was accepted in genuine love and respect. Regrettably, she was always in haste to leave on another journey, and her return visits spread further and further apart until eventually she ceased coming back altogether.

When his masters themselves died, their only child lost to the wilderness, Mahijah took their tiny house as his own and began trading food from the small garden under a side window for wool to create cloth. With much effort, and approaching his later years, he managed to gather a modest savings to support a family of his own. He found narrow contentment in marriage. His new bride, an ambitious, younger woman, quickly proved that her conjugal interests were essentially limited to his earning potential, viewing his skill with cloth as a way out of her own poverty. Nevertheless, his happiness grew as two children were added to their household, but was suddenly shattered when both of them, as well as his wife, died in yet another famine on the eve of his ninety-sixth year. This final straw, an ultimate loss to follow all previous losses, was too much for the man to bear, and his heart finally broke.

It was in the face of this most recent hurt, after wallowing in despair for many weeks, that Mahijah decided to leave the land of Sharon and start his life over far from the painful memories of his former dwellings. Regardless of the nearly constant sorrow he had experienced, he safeguarded a hopeful spark for a better life that would not be completely snuffed out. He arrived in the land of Haner and took over an abandoned house—no more than a shack, really—in the countryside, not far from the city that was still recovering from the invasion by Heni. He rounded up the last, lean, and lost sheep still grazing close by and, through innovation and hard work, turned them into a modest flock providing high quality wool for the clothing he sold to the war-weary inhabitants of his new nation. During one of his trips to the seller's market, he stumbled upon Jubal—begging in the streets—and learned of his history. He was instantly drawn to the younger man, and now considered him a fast friend.

"My thanks to you, my strong and faithful companion. Yes, many nights over many years did I toil by dim fire light, practicing my trade only after my other work was done," Mahijah replied. "Perchance one day before I die it will finally make me rich. Now *that*, for once, would be a *pleasant* turn of events!"

"I, too, aforetime desired riches," the musician all but murmured under his breath, slowing his steps to allow his companion to keep pace. Then, in full voice, he confessed, "Yes, I did once wish for gold, and copious quantities at that. I thought it would afford me all that I desired. A small chest of coins at first allowed me to move away from the home of my parents, marry my new love, and provide her with everything she could require. And, for a short time, life was good. We bought plenty to eat and plenty to entertain us. However, to our dismay, we soon discovered that the promise of gold was unfaithful. Even when abundant, it guaranteed neither friendship nor security. Easily was it taken, more easily was it spent, and ever were our thoughts upon it. The gods themselves were not given the devotion we offered to our gold, and the taste of my music grew bitter in my mouth because of it."

"The gods? I am surprised to hear you speak of them at all. From your stories, you have never given the gods their due," the cloak maker spoke skeptically, cautiously correcting his friend's narrative as they walked. Their footfalls landed lazily as they slowly strode through the boulevard, enjoying—as always—their cozy conversation. Neither of them was in a hurry to meet the rabble of the market. They would be thrown into the midst of it soon enough.

"Too true, my wise counselor," admitted Jubal with a small chuckle. "My late wife and I did keep our stone figurines on public display in our main room, a show for the praise of those we invited to our house. We even would ask favors of the statues from time to time, especially when we still wished to have children, but we never believed in their potency. As my father would say, 'Only a fool fashions a chunk of wood into the likeness of a chair and then worships it. The wiser man just sits.' "

He paused in the street, becoming as still as the silent idols he was describing. The thought of his abducted wife, likely killed, had stirred something inside him. Mahijah sensed his companion's mood swing and turned to face him, heedless of the travelers passing on either side. Jubal felt profound grief at the idea of Hannah's violent apprehension, rarely talking about her supposed fate, and having never spoken her name out loud since that dreadful day.

"How quickly the two of us lost our love!" Jubal continued, startled at his realization. "We were not married a full year before we become absent with each other, barely friendly. My parents were always happy, even in poverty. I can appreciate my despair at losing my wife to our raiders, and my parents and sisters to their machines of war. I can understand my sadness at losing my house and all my worldly riches. But all happiness had fled my soul long before our city ran from before its invaders. Tell me, you who have seen more years than I, is there hope that some of my lost joy will ever return?"

"Is that what you seek, my boy? Happiness?" Mahijah was probing in his reply. He knew that his friend had suffered long, more in his heart than in his body. Since the day they had first happened upon each other, he had been concerned for the young man's will to continue. Even the memory of his flute had not been able to awaken in Jubal a flame strong enough to survive on its own. Did the shepherd perceive a spark of hope yet burning inside his friend?

Without waiting for an answer, the older man continued. "Perhaps there is hope for some happiness yet to be, but I have little of my own to spare for you. Joy has not been a faithful companion to me. As you remember, my childhood was full of sorrow. Only here and there could I squeeze some delight out of it. I remember shadows of cheerfulness from being with my sister, then again from serving that generous couple until I buried them. Hard work once gave me pleasure, I confess, though I am rapidly losing that ability. Hunger, sickness, uncertainty, loneliness, betrayal, and shame: these have been my dependable confidants. I much prefer *your* loyalty. Though brief our acquaintance has been, I have always known you to be a kind man, wanting to be honest and true."

Mahijah slowly turned to continue their journey as an idea raced through his mind, an awareness he had never allowed full access to his consciousness until now. His head surged with wispy thoughts of seeking and wanting, trying to organize them into something coherent.

"That is it!"

Almost involuntarily, Mahijah spun around to face his friend again, stopping them both in the lane as before. Excitement swelled within his breast. With one hand he grabbed Jubal's shoulder, with the other hand he lifted Jubal's chin, forcing the artist to look directly at him. In those weary eyes the grayed man saw a glimpse of that which had just captivated his own mind and thrilled his very soul.

"What do you crave?"

Mahijah basically yelled the question, his hands shaking a little, a smile spreading across his face as he realized that he knew for himself the answer to his own question, convinced that his somber friend would soon know it, too.

"What is this? Has some demon suddenly possessed you? Loose me, I pray you. You frighten me!" Jubal called out as he stepped back, the shepherd's hands falling in front of him. He was not sure how to react to Mahijah's explosive inquiry. Jubal had never been scared of physical injury from the old man, and there was no fear in him now, but he was taken aback by the sudden change in the herdsman's demeanor. Something was obviously important to him.

"Apologies to you, Jubal. I lost myself for a moment. But oh what a moment!" the shepherd exclaimed excitedly. "I think I have an answer to your troubles—to our troubles—an answer that might just be within our grasps. Help me reason through my thoughts and maybe we can liberate ourselves this day. Tell me, what is it above all else that you desire?"

Jubal looked at his friend, then paused to seriously consider his question. "My soul is empty, and I am not sure why," he stammered, stepping forward with his own outstretched hand and clasping Mahijah by the forearm, staring down at the sand in the road. He thought intently, remembering his feelings of just a few minutes ago. "Yes, of course. I wish to be happy, as I suppose everyone does. But joy always seems to slip through my fingers. I have felt it from time to time, but never for very long. What will bring me lasting happiness?

"Years ago, I would have said that riches were the pathway to contentment, but I have since seen the folly in that. Gold cannot supply it, though most of my former companions claimed that gold was the answer to all of life's worries. It *did* give me pleasure for a season, but it also corrupted my mind and twisted my spirit, even before it vanished from my view. It was a pathetic source of happiness."

Jubal looked up from the road as he continued his reasoning. "Safety was always desirable, but rarely achieved in either the house of my childhood or in my own chambers once I was married. A painful accident or the withdrawal of good favor could take away my ability to work, and we all know from sad experience that security is as changeable as the whims of our warrior neighbors. My sunny childhood did not last, and the esteem of my parents slipped away as I aged. They are now dead, and—soon or late—I am bound to follow them to the grave. Nothing lasts. The one thing that has come the closest to giving me long-term satisfaction is my flute, but even the joy of making music has paled before my eyes. How do I fill my soul?"

"I have felt the same," spoke Mahijah dolefully, taking up the lament from his partner. "Have we not all felt it, across this city, throughout our land? We all seek a fullness in our lives, though we rarely find it. The rich are no better than the poor in this respect, for their gold cannot shield them from agony. As much as a strong body is a great tool, it cannot forever remain in good health. Back-breaking labor and sickness wear it out until death takes us. Tending flocks was once a pleasure for me, but work can only bring limited satisfaction before it grows stale. The praise of our fellows is unstable, conditioned upon making them feel better about their selfish activities. At my age, I have learned that memory becomes unreliable and intelligence dwindles as the mind grows soft and fatigued. And yet, we have both experienced some form of happiness, some shadow or gradation of it, though at present it might elude us."

Jubal agreed that he and his friend had both suffered, but that they had also both rejoiced, if to a lesser degree. His disheartening thoughts were hastily being replaced with something new and different. Already, the old man's words had stoked an ember of optimism within him, and his enthusiasm was growing. He saw the direction of their conversation and was eager to hurry headlong towards its conclusion.

"I see what you are saying, at least I believe I do. To be happy is what we both want—what everyone wants," the musician spoke tentatively at first, gaining confidence and urgency as his thoughts congealed. "Yes, this feels right, tastes true. But rather than passing happiness, we want the kind of joy that never ends, the type that extends beyond quick pleasures. As different as every person is from each another, we all want some similar satisfaction that supports who we are at our core, or at least who we want to become. Being true to ourselves, we long for a deep, cool well of happiness that will never dry up, a continuous supply of it like the air we breathe, living within us until our last breath. Durable happiness is what we seek, regardless of the circumstances in which we find ourselves. You and I both want a steady stream of joy, for now and for the future. It must be possible. All that we have to do is to find the source!"

Pleased that he had arrived at the same conclusion, Mahijah joined in his friend's earnestness. "Surely, there must be someone within our city that has found the spring of happiness. And if they are truly happy, they would want to share their discovery with others, would they not? Obviously they would, for it would increase their happiness to see it adorn the head of another. We have each learned our trades through training and effort, studying for ourselves and at the feet of those who have mastered them before us. Might we not extract from the masters of happiness the path they take to find joy, and walk in their footsteps?"

Out of pernicious habit, Jubal permitted some sinister doubt to creep into their conversation, becoming contrarian. "But this is a hard-hearted people, full of envy and hate and evil schemes. They love only their gold, trust only themselves, and serve only their lusts. Their whole existence depresses me, not exclusively due to their fraudulent folly, but because in the end I am one of them. We are all wicked and false."

Jubal's enthusiasm waned slightly as the insight sunk in, but he wanted to remain firm. He glanced at his counselor for encouragement, hoping the wiser man might counter his own fears. "No nation is *completely* evil, my young artist, just like no person is completely unhappy. There is always hope, even if hidden behind tremendous despair. Keep courage yet, and let me reflect."

Mahijah stroked his thin beard, straining his mind to think of someone—anyone—some group or troupe that might help him and his partner in their unexpected yet invigorating quest for lasting happiness. He was *sure* that, among all the residents he had encountered since arriving in the land, there would be at least one person who was both sincerely joyous *and* willing to act as a guide towards that joy.

Just then, a flurry of activity in the street roused the two friends from their private discourse, and they were once more aware of the crowds around them. Despite the hot sun, men and women and children were swarming in the byways. For some reason, everyone was rushing away from the center of the city and towards the western gate, shouting and questioning each other as they scurried about. It was not fright that exuded from the masses, but a nervous curiosity that seemed to propel them along as they pushed and shoved to get by each other. A preoccupied young girl bumped into Mahijah as she chatted with her companions, begging his pardon and trying to quickly move away, but he held out his hand to delay her for a moment.

"Where are you heading in such a hurry, my dear?" the shepherd asked delicately. "What has prodded our people to throng as they do, especially on such a warm day as today?"

"Have you not heard?" the girl replied, eager to explain her excitement. "*Everyone* is talking about it. There is a strange thing in the land. A seer is outside the city, screaming from the hills to the farmers and cattlemen about the gods and some imminent destruction. They sent word to us in the city, and we are going out to hear the news. My father says the outsider is warning of another war, and that we will all perish if we are attacked again, not being able to defend ourselves so soon after the last invasion. My brother says the ruckus is not about war at all, but concerns a drought that is soon to fall upon us. I do not know for sure, but we are all going to find out. A wild man has come among us!"

Mahijah's arm fell to his side as the girl raced off to catch up with her companions, apparently more interested in hearing something novel than in reflecting on what the message might be. A *seer*? A wild man crying in the wilderness? The words jogged an ancient recollection in the old shepherd's mind. He had heard of such things as a youth, but the memory was foggy, a shadow from days gone by. Yet it stirred something within his heart that would drive him, like the rest of the city, to hear the address being spoken from earthen heights.

"What did she say?" yelled Jubal, still by his side, the growing horde boiling around them. "Everyone looks agitated, edgy and captivated at the same time. Where are they going?"

Jubal motioned for Mahijah to move against one of the walls, away from the center of the street, and out of the strongest part of the frenzy. There they found some relief from the shoving and a chance to speak. The old man told his friend what little he knew.

"They are pushing to the western gate, outside the city," he said. "There is a crazy man, a preacher of some kind, warning of an approaching plague or some other disaster. More misery to fill our days, no doubt. It sounds terrible, but nevertheless I think we should go listen. I have an odd feeling about the whole thing."

And then Mahijah heard it in the throng, the name that would bring his muddled memories of the past into present clarity. He caught it first as a furtive whisper, so soft and rapid that he was unsure if he had heard it correctly. Then it came as a cautious question, laced with unbelief. Finally, he heard it as a choked shout above the din of the crowd.

"Zion!"

Of course! The memories came flooding back to the old man. *Zion*, the terrible city of burnings. Mahijah remembered now. *Zion*, the far away land of dragons and demons. Tales that his father would share around their small hearth flooded back to his mind—horrible stories, fearful accounts that would cause him to shiver. *Zion*, the people who could never be defeated in battle, who spewed fire and pestilence upon anyone who defied them. The savage name was the bane of every civilized society within the region.

The herdsman gave his second-hand version of the terrors of Zion to the musician, who had never heard the name. The accounts of a menacing, distant people had little effect on Jubal, in spite of his companion's animated retelling. Mahijah's disturbing description sounded exaggerated to him, like a ghost story used to scare children. Still standing against the wall, he was determined to pursue the joy that the shepherd had just barely convinced him they could find.

"Of sadness and destruction, we have had our fill. What need have we to hear more? Let us return to our sheep, as you would say, and not allow such things to distract us right now. Certainly not *now*, as we perceive ourselves on the verge of seeking a much greater reward. The crowd will unquestionably dwindle before too long, and we will resume our newly-initiated search for happiness."

Mahijah stood transfixed, intently scanning his memory, trying to understand why he had felt the need to join the crowd and to hear the words of the seer. He knew the flute player was correct. Without question, they did have a more noble interest to pursue than silly curiosity. But there was something elusive about that word *Zion*, and the shepherd could not let it go from his mind.

No. The word was not *only* terrible, perhaps not terrible or dreadful at all. Oddly, the more Mahijah pondered the word, the more optimistic and joyful he became. The concept of Zion, as vague as it was for him at present, made the shepherd feel warm inside, and a thin smile stole across his face. Conflicting memories sprouted in his mind, cheerful stories that he attributed to the old man and woman who had taken him into their home and saved him from starvation.

Then it hit him. The stories were actually not from the parents at all, but from their child—from the girl. He remembered the scraps of travel tales from the couple's traveling daughter—she who had always beamed like a clear, sunny day when arriving at their house, but who had always wept like a rain-swelled sky when departing from it. Zion, she told her parents, was a glorious place, a city of love and kindness, a society of wealth beyond measure and safety beyond comprehension. She had happened upon it during one of her journeys in the desert, learned of its culture, and decided to accept its philosophies. Within its gates, she built a house with the help of welcoming friends who accepted her as family.

The gods lived among its people. It was a city of friendship and peace where everyone lived in harmony and helped out before they were even asked. Love, laughter, prosperity, and music filled its avenues, having chased away apathy, anger, poverty, and dread. Every noble craft and trade found full expression within its walls, a border that seemed to have room for all who wished to enter its gates. But there was no space for greed, villainy, or hate inside its boundaries. Nor was hunger known among its occupants, for its grain was bounteous and its fruit plentiful.

On each visit home, the daughter invited her parents to give up their meager lives in favor of living fully with her inside the borders of her new nation, but mother and father ever resisted, being unable to accept that such a place could exist. They were focused exclusively on their demands that she return to live with them again, that she assist with their labors to survive, and that she wed a young man from the local population. Her wanderings through the wilderness were troubling to them, and they would not listen to her accounts. Their deafness to her pleas caused the girl the only type of sadness she was still able to experience.

"Zion!" Mahijah himself shouted, looking the younger man in the eyes. "This is it! Jubal, we must see this seer."

With confident strides, the cloak maker moved to rejoin the mob, abruptly grabbing by the hand his friend who stumbled alongside him, surprised by the old man's strength. The shepherd continued to explain, the smile on his face growing larger as they hurried along.

"This wild man, the seer, he surely has the answer to our pursuit. I have heard of his city. It is a place of prosperity and security, of justice and compassion. Its people is full of happiness if ever such a society could exist. They know the secret to lasting joy. This prophet will teach us how to achieve our deepest desire. He will be our salvation."

"How can you know this?" Jubal struggled to equal the pace of his aged partner, but was convinced he must keep up with him. He knew the shepherd to be both rational and restrained, and was certain that Mahijah would not rush into some untried situation without good cause. The old man's grief-stricken, former years had given him a measured demeanor. Never before had Jubal witnessed him so intent, so confident. But there was more to it. Mahijah seemed more alive, happier than Jubal had ever known him to be. Strangely, the musician himself was beginning to feel the same way.

"Praise the gods! My heart sings. My mind is ablaze. I am not sure exactly how I know, but I am convinced the seer will direct us aright. We must hear his words," the herdsman rejoiced.

"Yes, you are right. I feel it, too," said the flute player, startled to hear his own reply. The excitement of pursuing happiness multiplied within him as he contemplated the concept of Zion, gripping the hand of his friend more tightly. He was undoubtedly feeling the same exhilaration that the old man had described. With a smile of his own unconsciously forming on his face, he finished his response.

"It is an extraordinary sensation, the likes of which I have rarely if ever felt before, but I cannot deny it. I also wish to hear what we will about this peculiar city and its occupants. To the wild man we must go!"

And so the companions hurried towards the west, faces shining with anticipation as they melted into the multitude of impatient spectators. Something strange had truly arrived in the land.

Intuitively, the musician and the shepherd welcomed it.

HAPPINESS IS OUR DEEPEST DESIRE

2

FREE TO CHOOSE

JUBAL WAS RESOLUTE. BY THE time he and his friend, Mahijah the shepherd, cleared the still fragmented gates of their once fine city, he had become more determined than ever to reach the small hill that graced the gentle slopes of Haner and to join the expanding crowd that was already gathering there. His face still bore the smile it had formed as he spoke with his friend mere minutes ago.

Could it be true? he thought, stealing a glance at the old man next to him and finding his friend—ever gripping his hand—returning an even wider smile. There was growing hope in that wrinkled face, and Jubal felt the same hope swelling within his own soul.

The companions were hastening to hear the words of an itinerant preacher, a wild man and purported seer, who had stationed himself outside their city. Rumors in the streets alleged that he had journeyed from Zion, the mysterious land of demons and death. Mahijah had heard of the perils of Zion as a child at the feet of his father, nearly a hundred years ago, but he felt no dread now as he rushed to listen to one of its leaders. On the contrary, the very mention of the name Zion filled his heart with peace and joy, a feeling he could not yet explain but which he very much wanted to last. Perhaps this was because he remembered a contrarian history, told by an adopted older sister whom he barely knew, which rang more true to him: that Zion was actually a place of prosperity and love.

In any event, hearing the name *Zion* had caused excitement and reverence to sprout within Mahijah's breast, emotions equivalent to those experienced by his younger ally. They both felt an odd happiness, their hearts filling with courage and confidence, their minds brimming with the burgeoning belief that the teachings of Zion might be a salve to their gloomy souls. So they had abandoned their plans to visit the marketplace today, and instead determined to hear the evangelist atop the gentle hill just a short, dusty walk from the western gate.

To call the rotting and charred ruins of what once was Haner's door to the setting sun a *gate* was generosity approaching dishonesty. It had lost every hint of its former integrity. All that remained of the once proud barrier of thick boards attached to thicker walls were crumbled pieces of stone and sorry splinters of wood, too small to serve as kindling for a pauper's fire. The strong planks of seasoned lumber were all broken or burned, ripped from the metal moorings that fastened them to the stone of the adjacent walls. No trace was left of the decorative carvings that once adorned the entrance, lost to history and fading from the memories of the residents who still dared to call the ruined city their home. The same was true of the other three doors, each facing one of the cardinal directions. Despite a twenty percent levy imposed on all their goods, there were in the city men and materials sufficient to make repairs to the barriers, but Haner was no longer free to do so. Their king was dead—executed—and their new overlords insisted, as a daily reminder of their mastery over the city, that the gates not be repaired.

Circumstances had been quite different in this ancient valley of moderate rain and abundant sunshine scarcely two years earlier. Haner was a fairly populous city then, with healthy farmlands surrounding its walls and a bustling marketplace within them. Servants did the majority of the menial labor. Commoners focused on work suitable to their station: shoeing horses, repairing dwellings, building simple wooden conveniences for the wealthy, farming, raising cattle, and the like. The rich were few enough in number to accentuate their superiority. The majority of them inherited their silver and gold, while a middling pushed their way into the upper ranks with skill and effort. The king was only moderately corrupt, relying on a dependable stream of taxes. He was satisfied to enforce his will or outright steal from his subjects only when uncomfortable pressure was brought to bear. Everyone was content with the safety they supposed the mighty walls of their city afforded.

It was at that time that the arrival of an invading army caused Haner's king severe discomfort. Wars between neighboring cities were common—almost expected—as a means to increasing wealth through conquest. Haner had not fallen prey to such an attempt for a while and, with ample time and resources to prepare, should have been able to resist the onslaught. But it was not. After a siege of forty days, the aggressors from Heni breached its defenses and scattered its residents, killing over half of its military forces. The people of Haner were spared, but only so they could return to their homes and lands as subjects to their new masters, submitting to a heavy tax.

"Yes, it is true!" Mahijah shouted, answering the unspoken question he could sense on the face of his young companion. He was obligated to raise his voice to be heard above the din of the throng that now surrounded them in the road outside the city.

Even while under foreign oppression, the lure of Haner's marketplace was tempting enough to fill the public square with customers, especially on the first day of the week. But the streets of the city and the roads leading from it had rarely been this busy. It appeared as if the entire populace was spilling out its western gate. Jubal and Mahijah were enveloped by strangers and loose acquaintances, all seemingly as intent as were the friends to ascend the low mount and listen to the seer's message. Mahijah wondered if the others also felt the odd longing to hear about the strange and magnificent City of Zion and the unending happiness of its blessed inhabitants.

The two pilgrims had only been friends for the last five months. Jubal grew up within the walls of Haner, never leaving its bounds in his thirty-eight years. The strong and affable son of a carpenter, he learned to play the flute while a child, and applied himself to the hobby with such diligence over the course of his life that he became quite famous. Famous and *rich*. That was until his city was besieged and overthrown, his wife and parents killed, and his already declining fortunes utterly ruined. From that point forward, he began begging in the streets, surrendering to despair and loneliness, refusing to make music again.

In the land of Sharon, Mahijah had also experienced harsh misfortune, losing to sickness, famine, and greed first his mother, then the remainder of his large family, and eventually a wife and children of his own. His firm mind and generally upbeat attitude fared better under these conditions than his lanky though feeble frame, but not by much. With his thin beard grayed, he tried to leave his sorrows behind by parting from his homeland and taking up residence outside of Haner, just after the invasion by Heni's army. Since then, he survived by raising a small flock of sheep and sewing a few cloaks, befriending Jubal on one of his trips to the city's center to sell his cloth and coverings in the marketplace.

The two strangers considered their new friendship a mutual benediction. Jubal relied on the advice and kindness of his wise ally and had begun ever so slowly to shed his melancholy as a result of receiving them. Mahijah depended on the strength and passion of his younger partner, enjoying the tales and perspective from his much different life, and anticipating one day to hear many songs from his custom-made pan flute that was so dearly cherished.

"Stay with me. Stay close. I see a place just ahead where we can rest," Jubal encouraged his friend as they drew nearer to the end of their short, unexpected trek.

Very soon, they arrived at the base of the low hill and stepped aside the path at a level location to catch their breaths in the hot sun. They were still a decent distance from the top of the earthen rise, but could plainly see the figure of a man standing tall at its crest, facing a large and spreading crowd slightly below him.

The travelers were too far away to clearly hear what the man was preaching, but it obviously had an arousing effect on his audience. The evangelist would speak for a few minutes, holding his listeners in stunned silence until he stopped. Then the crowd would react with an uproar, fists pumping in the air and faces scowling with anger. Sometimes the mob's vitriol was so profound towards the man that they would start to press towards him, threatening with their staves to beat him into silence. But the missionary seemed undeterred by their intimidations. Each hateful wave that approached quickly dissolved—how or by what means they were repelled was impossible to tell from where the pilgrims stood—and the preacher persisted in his message. It was a sight to inspire awe.

A steady stream of new onlookers was making the hike up the hill to join the mob. As Jubal watched, he noticed some of them had started their upward trek from a spot not many steps to the north, leaving behind a group of assembled tents and attentive servants tasked with guarding them. It looked as if the servants were observing from afar the progress of their masters and the related events, as best that they could. To the perspiring artist, the protection of the canvassed stalls was inviting.

"Come, this way," Jubal said to the herdsman, who was leaning on his arm, still struggling with the heat of the day and his recent exertions. "Let us take rest in the shade of those tents and hear what their keepers can tell us of this affair."

The musician and the shepherd slowly advanced until they stood in front of the tent-keepers. They received a friendly welcome from the nearest of the company, who allowed them to take shelter in the door of his master's temporary porch. They thanked him, then pressed him for details regarding the preacher. Not only was the tent's guardian kind, but he was full of helpful information that he had accumulated throughout the day, regarding the spectacle on the mount.

He explained that the stranger had arrived a little less than four hours earlier, entering the city to announce himself and his message before taking a position at the top of the small hill. News of the arriving wild man spread slowly at first through the streets of Haner. The servant's master, being among the initial inhabitants to hear the tidings, gathered friends about him to go and see, bringing tents to shade them from the merciless heat. In this way, the prophet's audience started as only a handful of people, but quickly blossomed into hundreds as word of his presence infiltrated the city.

And, as far as the servant could tell, it was still growing, though at a slower rate. The original arrivals had started to leave, becoming exhausted in the desert sun and apparently returning to whatever their previous activities of the day had been, but his master was still on the hill.

"Who is the man?" Mahijah questioned their host. "Do you know his name and if he truly travels from Zion? What news does he have to share with our poor city? My heart tells me he brings peace."

"I have not been up to see for myself, as I must tend to the tent," the servant replied, "and none of our party has come back down from listening to him. I have overheard mumblings from the residents returning to the city, but they react so differently that it is hard for me to understand what is happening. For all I have observed, there may be three or four separate preachers delivering completely different messages at the top of that hill, though I confess there is but one of them in view."

"How can that be?" queried Jubal, squinting his eyes towards the earthen rise, impatient to know some piece of reliable information about the minister and his message. When still within the bounds of the city, he and Mahijah had heard of only one preacher, the wild man.

"Some who have listened are fearful, saying the man is a devil who will conjure a plague to destroy us all if we don't chase him away. They bemoan unavoidable war and famine, unable to be consoled by their companions," the servant continued. "Others are angry, either fuming that he is a fool babbling about nothing at all, or pronouncing curses upon him and swearing to deploy soldiers to arrest him for his insults. They say he should be stoned before he causes a real problem. Others wear shocked looks on their faces, saying nothing. Some few are oddly happy and at peace, bounding down the mount full of laughter and excitement, smiling—even singing—as they declare that we must all listen to the man, that we should gather families and friends to come and see. It is too confusing for me. Will you go listen, then return to me here to share the truth of it all?"

"We shall see," stated Jubal candidly, expressing gratitude to the tent-keeper again for his help. "Come, Mahijah, we have rested long enough. We must hear for ourselves before the preacher turns away."

Their steps were light as the friends began their walk up the slope, that same feeling of happiness, which they had felt back in the city, blooming within them without explanation. By this time, the downward tide of humanity had strengthened, giving the perception that the sermon was nearing its end. The pilgrims quickly neared the crowd, the younger assisting the older, then softly pressed through it until they were close enough to see the speaker. Expectations were high as they stood side by side, viewing him for the first time.

He was surprisingly average in appearance—unremarkable really—as he stood relaxed before the crowd, obviously waiting for their most recent tirade to subside. Other than his calm manner in facing the mob, nothing about him was odd or extraordinary as far as the friends could tell. He was a younger man, near to the age of Jubal in appearance, with an unmistakable presence of health and integrity about him. He actually stood shorter than he had appeared from a distance, not quite as tall as Mahijah, though straight and poised. His garment was a commoner's mantle, tidy and kempt, though stained with dust from the roads he had traveled, its hood blowing with the occasional breeze. Simple sandals adorned his otherwise bare feet. At his toes in a heap lay what looked like a worn satchel, sturdy and large, with a long strap to throw about the shoulder. A wineskin, only half full, lay next to it. No coin purse could be seen on his person. On his face he wore a light brown beard, just long enough to cover his chin.

He could have passed for any number of men in the streets of Haner, except for one distinguishing feature: his faced beamed with a relentless, forgiving grin that defied the abusive words and bodily threats regularly emanating from his audience. It was almost as if light shined from his smile. That *alone* set him apart from anyone Jubal had previously met in his entire life, and yet he still had not heard the man speak. Fortunately, the crowd's fresh outburst was beginning to dwindle.

Without warning, Mahijah pushed away from his friend's side and stepped forward from the crowd, boldly walking to within two paces of the preacher. The man halted his discourse in mid-sentence and the fervor of the crowd subsided. The slope of the hill at its crest was such that the cloak maker was forced to raise his eyes a little to meet those of the seer. He pulled himself to his full height, looked the prophet straightly in the eye, and unashamedly asked that which had burned within him but could not be answered earlier by the tent-keeper.

"Tell us plainly who you are, and from where you have come. Tell us how to be forever happy."

The preacher stood in silence, continuing to smile, intrigued by the shepherd's plea. Already he had delivered his message several times, having spoken by now for many hours to an ever-changing group of listeners, but he was willing to respond to the herdsman. In fact, he seemed pleased to at last receive a sincere question after experiencing what must have been a constant flow of hate and complaining so far that afternoon. He lowered both hands to his sides with palms up, in a gentle gesture of welcome.

"I am Enoch, son of Jared, descended from Adam. Silver and gold have I none, but such as I have, I will give. I have come from Zion, a holy city where the righteous rejoice day upon day. While traveling through the land, the Lord showed me a vision and commanded that I speak the truths of it to all I would encounter. He is my God and yours. You are my brothers and sisters, but you seek to counsel our Counselor. Repent instead and, through the mercy of our Creator, find both forgiveness and the happiness you desire."

Mahijah sank to the ground, fumbling with his hands for a stone upon which to sit while keeping his eyes on the speaker. He finally found one and sat upon it, ever giving watchful heed to Enoch as he continued his preaching. Jubal crawled up to sit beside him and they both listened intently, transfixed.

This is what they had hoped to hear! The prophet spoke of love and compassion, claiming that everlasting happiness was their inheritance if only they would live in such a way to find it. The path would be difficult but rewarding, a way to develop into the most fulfilled person either of them could hope to become. The minister recounted the joy of the saints, those who lived in Zion and labored to do what was best for themselves and their neighbors.

It was a simple, tender faith, free from the paralyzing dogma associated with the stone gods popular in Haner. As Enoch spoke, he seemed to ignore the larger crowd and focus only on the two seated pilgrims who hung on every word. Here and there, they would turn to each other and smile or nudge each other knowingly. At times, they would have a question, but dared not interrupt for fear of missing the next important point of the address. They lost track of time as their focus remained fixed on the seer.

After a while, Enoch made his final appeal to the larger audience and stopped speaking, indicating that his lesson was finished for the day. He took a long draught from his wineskin, a few drops of water dripping down his mouth, then bade everyone goodbye.

By now the mob had dwindled, and, with the scene ended, the remaining spectators pivoted back to the east, returning towards the city and leaving him alone on the hill. As they retired, he slowly gathered his meager possessions, took a last look back at Haner, and made as if to walk down the northern slope of the hill and away from the city.

"Wait!" cried Jubal, rising from the ground and reaching a hand out to Enoch. "*Please*, wait," he implored again, softening his tone and reaching with his other hand to help Mahijah get up from his seat. "Are you done so soon? We have only just begun to understand your words."

Enoch turned back to face the voice that had summoned him, willing to patiently delay his departure a few minutes more. The flute player was still helping the shepherd rise, sore from sitting on the ground and looking upward for so long. The seer waited until they were both erect.

"What would you ask of me?" he inquired, bending at the waist to lay his satchel back on the ground, then straightening to give the friends his full attention.

Jubal blurted out his request in a single breath, as the cloak maker nodded in agreement. "Please, master. We recognize that you are a man of God. Your words have burned within us and we know that you speak the truth. How grateful we are that you have blessed our land with your sojourn. We are not sure how to repay your generosity. Before you depart, do tell us how we can be rich like you."

For just a moment, Enoch's face turned grim. He was all too acquainted with the evil that lurks in the hearts of men. On his journeys, he had encountered plenty of conspiring and malicious onlookers pretending to be devoted disciples, but then revealing their actual intentions. He branded such folk as wolves in sheep's clothing, but was that a fair label for the two listeners in front of him now? He took a deep breath and closed his eyes, as if considering their case like an upright judge. His smile returned as he exhaled and reopened his eyes, realizing that his residual questioners were most likely sincere. He decided to test their motives to be positive.

"You want riches, do you? I have spoken to you of neither silver nor of gold, my friends, though my people do possess all the money they could ever desire. Your ears must be tired and your minds hot from the afternoon sun. Return to your homes and consider the true meaning of what I have spoken."

"No, not money," Jubal was embarrassed by his poor choice of words. "I did not mean the wealth one finds in the palace of a king. I have known those treasures: fine linen and clothing, sumptuous feasts, precious jewels, and chests of gilded plunder. I meant the riches that spring from within, which you most evidently possess. How can we hold onto this feeling of joy that brightens your visage, which flows from your mouth and gives our hearts song?"

"So what you *really* desire is not gold, but happiness. You have been taught by others that gold *is* happiness, but of course that counsel is falsehood. You have heard me speak of my people, those who are truly and fully happy. Do you wish to be like them?" Enoch looked directly at the two friends, curious to hear their reply.

"Yes, that is what we desire!" Jubal exclaimed without delay. "Will you take us to your city to visit its inhabitants, that we might learn how to be happy as you are?"

The preacher made an exaggerated motion of looking around the hill, to the left hand and to the right, then between his questioners as if they might be hiding other listeners behind them. For the first time, he seemed a little dejected, turning his gaze down the hill towards the receding mob which was growing ever smaller in the distance. There were no more tents standing north of the footpath entering the city, their masters and their keepers having retreated inside the gate.

"Are there but two listeners, in a land of thousands, with ears to hear?" Enoch moaned his query, more to the heavens than to the companions. Then, turning to scrutinize his audience of two, he offered a warning. "You are asking a hard thing without appreciating the cost of it. The path to happiness is little traveled, requiring courage and stamina. Do you not understand that I am hated by all I meet? Falsehoods precede my every sermon, each nation I encounter cursing my name with disgust and fear. You cannot truly wish to remain in my company, nor to become like others of the same ilk. If you do, you risk receiving the same treatment and becoming a pariah in the land."

"How can men or women hate you? There has been nothing in your words to provoke fury," Mahijah confirmed his friend's declaration with fervor, unwilling to let the prophet make a pretense to deny their request. "We care nothing for the shame they hurl. Can we not accompany you to Zion?"

Enoch smiled, glanced up at the firmament for the last time, and then returned his regard to his questioners, satisfied by their responses. "I commend you for your integrity," he began with a sincere compliment, then proceeded to answer the direct question. "Oh, I do not really think that they hate me *personally*, for they hardly know me at all. We cannot love or hate those who are strangers to us, but only despise that which we think they represent—or worse, ignore them altogether. I am just a convenient scapegoat. Their sins accuse them and they are uncomfortable with my words. But of all the occupants of Haner, you two are the only ones who have paused to thank me this day. For that, I applaud you, and offer my own gratitude in return.

"However, I cannot take you to Zion at present, for I have further lands to visit before I have fulfilled the mandate given me. Now, the daylight is waning and I must away before darkness falls. Nonetheless, you can discover Zion yourselves, for it is no secret to those seeking to find it. Follow the line of my arm a journey of six days to the south. The way is strait and will surely prove arduous for the weak-hearted. Continue in faith and, on the seventh day, you shall find rest."

Enoch gestured with his right arm towards the south, beyond other hills and to a land out of sight. He waited as his two hearers visibly hesitated at first, then reluctantly turned to look in the direction he had indicated. He could tell that their hopes were dampened by his response; it was evidently less gratifying than what they had expected. The prophet felt a tinge of sorrow at not being able to serve them straightaway in the manner they desired.

"Wait," he spoke tenderly, now *his* turn to ask an indulgence of *them*. "I can see that both of you are genuine in your pursuit. The day dims for all of us the same, and you will not want to leave on such an expedition to be caught in the dark unprepared. Return to your dwellings tonight and make ready your beasts, provisions, shelters, and all other supplies you will need for the passage. Take rest until the morning, then onward to Zion with the daylight. Do not hesitate nor delay your travels, for the joy you have felt will fade if left unheeded. When promptings present themselves, actions must follow. Words and intentions alone are insufficient."

He could tell that his authentic concern towards them for a fruitful, rewarding trip was appreciated, but their enthusiasm was still slow to recover, significantly lower than its peak level from earlier in the afternoon. Enoch thought he might contribute an extra admonition to boost their spirits and see them through to the dawning of the next day.

"And one more thing, something further to consider tonight as you make your preparations. I will share with you one of the fundamental keys to Zion's happiness, its prosperity and success. It is among the first truths, a foundation upon which—of necessity—all other principles are built. It is a belief that you did not hear me preach today as you sat on your rock. And with it, I will give you an admonition."

The seer briefly interrupted himself, giving his new friends space to grasp the significance of what he was about to say. They unconsciously inclined forward, awaiting the grand reveal as a seeker of treasure holds her breath in anticipation of spying her prize for the first time.

"Freedom." Though it fell quietly from Enoch's lips, the single word seemed to echo about the hill. Already the pilgrims were once more captivated by their teacher.

"Each of us is the person we choose to become, and we are all free to make that choice," explained the prophet a bit more fully.

"How is that?" asked Mahijah, a confused expression spreading across his face as he looked to Enoch for more details, then glanced at his companion, and then stared back towards the preacher. Jubal was equally muddled by the declaration, though he kept silent in anticipation of a forthcoming answer.

The prophet did not immediately respond, but took the wineskin from off his shoulder and laid it next to his satchel. He cleared pieces of brush from the ground in front of him, then squatted down on his heels facing his tiny audience, arms resting on his thighs. He beckoned them to join him on the ground where he could better see their faces, and they both willingly complied, like children eager for their first day of school.

"Happiness is a conscious selection, my friends," Enoch reiterated, "and we possess an intrinsic independence to act as we judge best. The wisdom of this is obvious to the observant. In every circumstance we find ourselves, we are able to decide how to react to the situation—to be happy about it, or not. You have seen this standard in your personal lives, among your family and friends, even among strangers. When the weather turns cold, a young girl will rejoice that mountain snow is around the corner, while her sister will complain that she now needs to gather more firewood to keep warm. For both sisters the situation is the same: it is getting colder, and they will each experience snow in the mountains while requiring more wood for the fire. However, one is happy and the other is sad. How can this be possible?"

His friends nodded in comprehension, but were content to let Enoch unfold his message without immediate interruption.

"It is because one girl made the choice to be happy, and the other chose to be sad. No matter where or when we find ourselves in this existence, all of life is a choice: what to eat, what to wear, how to earn wages, who to marry, how to worship God. We decide to be honest in the marketplace with our customers or to steal from our neighbors by word or deed. We elect to flee from our enemies, or to fight them, or to turn our cheek for another blow. We elect to repent of our mistakes and to forgive those who have trespassed against us—or not. We all make choices and reap the rewards or pains of those judgements. In all our choosing, we are responsible for the outcomes. This is how life has been from the very beginning. God gave options for behavior to our first parents, compelling them to choose which ones they wished to pursue, with attendant rewards and penalties following.

"In the midst of all our daily choices, we must resolve to become the best possible version of ourselves that we can. Some decisions are strictly trivial, but being honest and straightforward in our hearts is an essential election. We should recognize who we are now and agree to be a better person tomorrow. Our personal integrity directs us like an inward light, guiding us in our choices to do only those things that will result in our joy. We make these virtuous decisions with full freedom, for not even our Creator will deign to force us against our will. He leaves the verdicts of our individual lives to each of us, offering options throughout our existence to see what we will make of ourselves. It is a liberating principle."

"So, what if we cannot make our own choices, if our situation constricts or constrains us in overpowering ways, preventing us from being our proper masters?" Jubal probed, trying to understand Enoch's teaching.

"Such as in a small child being subject to parents who tell her all the day long what chores to do, where to go, and when to sleep?" the evangelist clarified. "Or do you mean the mature among us who *behave* like children: the sick, or the injured, or those otherwise unable to sufficiently understand what they are doing? Such people are not expected to choose prudently, for their minds are not yet—or no longer—capable of comprehending the significance of their actions. They are not accountable for their conduct. The earnest, though limited, efforts they make in light of their condition effectively fill the measure of their existence. We should serve them, ensuring that they receive the most benefit from their lives, but we need not pity them. The promise is certain that they will receive the same happiness as those who are competent to make informed decisions, who have chosen righteously. The Creator assures us of this.

"Or rather yet, Jubal, do you mean to ask what responsibility we carry if, as reasoning adults, we are forced to do something against our will? Do we bear blame if our choice is less than free? What if the king holds us in his inner keep in a time of distress, preventing us from saving the lives of our parents and sisters, or of our disaffected wife?"

Jubal shot up to his feet, alarmed that this stranger could know such intimate details from the latest war, which he alone from among his family had survived. He glared at Mahijah, for a moment suspecting that his gray companion had somehow whispered facts regarding his tragic story to their host. But it was immediately plain to see that the herdsman was as shocked as his artistic ally. The flute player stood in icy silence, hesitant about what to do next.

"Peace, my friend," Enoch calmed Jubal's distress with his soothing tone, convincing him to return to his seat on the ground. "Your companion has not betrayed you. The small voice within me has revealed pieces of your past, some of your struggles and passions. I know of the losses you endured two years ago, and of the despair that has filled your heart up until today. As the combat was joined and your king held you prisoner in his palace, you were not completely able to make decisions for yourself. Someone had forced you into a circumstance that was largely beyond your control. Tell me, what choice did you have in that?"

"Well, none at all, I suppose," Jubal stammered. "The lord of Haner would not let me return to my house, nor send for word of my wife's situation. I was trapped at his palace and required to play my flute at his whim, unable to prevent her capture by the soldiers of Heni. Nor could I remove my parents and sisters away from the perils of the outer wall and to the greater security of my house. They were crushed when the invaders broke through our defenses. Back in the inner keep, I was safe for a time, I confess, but would much have preferred to risk my life for my family."

"You begin to see the importance of the freedom I mentioned," said the prophet, grasping a smooth stick from the hillside between his hands. "Of course, in that condition there were some things you could not do. Your assortment of options was restricted and you had to settle for decisions that were less than ideal. It is a sad tale, no doubt, but comparable to what we each encounter at some level all the days of our lives. The uncertainty of our existence leads us through winding roads and unpredictable paths, compelling us to make the most of what we are given.

"In the end, we are always at liberty to select how to act in our hearts. While the king's prisoner, did you do your utmost to serve him with your music? Did you encourage him to do that which was best for his subjects? Did you buoy the spirits of his soldiers, helping give them confidence before a terrible enemy? Did you attend to those who fell sick? No man—no god—can take from us our ultimate choices. Even if buried under the weight of this very hill upon which we sit, we could decide to be cheerful with our fate. One day, you may conclude that your tale is not as wretched as you had thought, and that the element of chance was an illusion used to explain what could not be appreciated. We are as free as we choose to be."

"These are hard words to hear," said Mahijah in frustration. He had become a little agitated at Enoch's speech and it was now his turn to interject. "Never have I listened to someone talk as you do, not in nearly one hundred years. Surely, the king might have power to make choices and be at liberty to come and go as he pleases, but how are we free? Our taxes alone make us slaves to cruel masters."

"Yes, my shepherding friend, these words can definitely be hard. The absent multitudes typically think as much, as I warned you before," the seer responded mildly, stirring the dirt at his feet with one end of the stick. "But have you not been free in your life? Did you not choose to serve the old couple, to marry and have children, and to leave the boundaries of Sharon for a fresh start in the land of Haner?"

With his words, Enoch gave Mahijah a shock akin to the one Jubal had just received, though the old man was content to remain in his place. Evidently, the seer was able to understand much of what they had suffered. Undoubtedly, he would be enlightened enough to guide them aright.

"Despite oppressive taxes and the tyranny of your conquerors, you enjoy much freedom, though the king does possess a larger chunk in some respects, exercising control and dominion over his subjects as you mentioned. Personal liberty to feel, to think, to speak, and to act allows us to chart a path for our lives that leads to contentment. It can never be fully restricted. We are responsible before ourselves, our fellow beings, and our God for how we behave along that path. All too frequently, we employ our individual freedom to select an improper path, to make bad decisions, or to create malevolent works. Without question we are responsible for our sinful judgements as much as our moral ones, and will undeniably face the consequences—at times the painful penalties—of each. Since people overwhelmingly prefer reward to punishment, the sweet taste of happiness usually results in a robust, palpable impulse to enlarge our cheerful consumption through virtuous verdicts of our own selection.

"Freedom is entwined with virtue—and vice—for the later can only be created when people possess the former. Liberty is among the most powerful combatants of iniquity, for it unleashes the good that may then oppose evil. When there is trouble in our world, a foul problem to be solved or nasty persecution to overcome, the solution is almost inevitably a hefty dose of freedom. But compulsion is abhorrent to our Maker. He will not force us to do his will, nor to bask in his fullness. It is the persuasive voice, the convincing tale, or the gentle admonition that respects a person's independence to make her own resolutions and to arrive at her own measured conclusions.

"You see, the freer we are the happier we can be. My people have joined with me in building our city for this very reason. Lasting happiness is only available to those who are lastingly free. My people wanted to be as happy as possible and yearned for their ethical choices to deliver the most significant impact. So they resolved to live in a place that would allow for the most liberty imaginable, the most independence available. Zion is the freest city on earth."

"And as their leader, you must be the richest man on earth," Jubal blurted, again thinking less of the silver and gold that undoubtedly fills the bolted coffers of a free nation—purged of kings who would tax and oppress them—and more of the riches of the eternal worlds.

"Though only one of their mortal rulers, I am indeed rich. Richer than all the kings of this world. For I am the poorest man in Zion."

Jubal pondered the contrast. How could the missionary be rich and poor at the same time? It was a question for future contemplation, for although he and his companion had remained enthralled for every second of their private sermon, he was growing tired, and was convinced the cloak maker was feeling the same way.

Enoch also perceived that his listeners were becoming weary, and decided that he should be on his way. He slowly stood, wiping the dirt that had accumulated about his cloak and sandals, shooing an insect from around his face. Practiced motions placed his bag and wineskin to his shoulders, betraying decades of repetition.

"I thank you for our conversation and wish we could continue. Alas, the hour is far spent, and we must part—me to my next engagement, and you to your arrangements for tomorrow. I thrill at the thought of your new adventure about to begin. Which leaves only the promised warning."

The friends rose gradually from the earth, stiff from sitting though warm from the nourishment they had received.

"Remember I told you that the less restricted we are, the more happy we may become?" the seer asked as both students nodded in agreement, recalling Enoch's instruction. "My warning is this: there is a great hazard in being free, for the more free we are, the more miserable and desperate we may become."

"Say that again," Mahijah insisted, sure he had misheard. "Did you not just tell us that freedom *was* happiness, or rather that freedom to choose *leads* to happiness? Are you trying to confuse this poor old man?"

"It is a massive challenge—a danger of sorts—that I leave with you. Yes, freedom is our birthright. It belongs to us, and along with it, the ability to choose. But happiness is only ours if we select actions leading to it. We are equally free to possess misery, fear, and doubt if we make decisions leading to them. The magnitude of our joy or distress is based upon how free we are. This is why some people prefer to linger in their chains, becoming comfortable with them and satisfied with the limited happiness they afford. For although people in such a condition have cut themselves off from greater happiness, at least they will neither experience greater grief. Our fates are in our own hands, for better or for worse. I pray you will choose wisely. Fare you well."

The prophet parted from his pupils, pushing slow footfalls down the northern slope of the unnamed hill, venturing towards whichever nation he would visit next. The pilgrims were left standing behind him, motionless, marveling at what had just transpired. The artist and the cloak maker remained strangely still, watching him fade into the distance until he disappeared over the horizon. Without a word, they turned towards each other, clearly discerning the appreciation and resolve that radiated from the other.

The musician spoke first, his voice quivering. "I am Jubal. I am my father's son, but I am not determined by the actions of my father. I remember being in his presence and listening to his teachings. I look back on his actions, seeing how he led his life, testing his decisions against my own heart. I make my own choices. I take the bad and toss it to the wind. I take the good and clutch it close to my breast. I decide who I am, who I am to become. I am my own master, free to do as I will, free to joy in the life that is mine, and free to suffer when I betray those principles that lead to happiness. I choose love. I choose a better life."

Jubal considered the full weight of what he had said—what he was about to say. "I choose to seek Zion."

The shepherd, surprised by his companion's declaration, could not help but be caught up in the reverence and zeal that accompanied it. "I am Mahijah. I am your friend. I choose to make your journey my own."

FREEDOM
EMPOWERS CHOICE

3

ONE HEART AND ONE MIND

JUBAL WAS ANXIOUS. FOR THE first time in two years he had risen before the sun. Sitting in the pre-dawn gloom on the straw of his makeshift bed, he absently stroked his cherished pan flute, running his fingers back and forth across the nine pipes of various sizes. He was impatient to be away.

No, he corrected himself, *impatient* was not quite right. More than impatient, he was giddy. It was similar to how he had felt on those once-frequent occasions when he and his deceased wife invited local nobles to their spacious residence. Their sole objective was to impress vain guests with their latest acquisition of fashionable wines, and in their lightmindedness they snickered at the platitudes carelessly tossed at them.

But that was not quite accurate either. He was not drunk. It was a different kind of lightheadedness. Nor was the emotion fleeting or superficial. He struggled to describe it, but then he recognized the feeling. It was *happiness*, and it was unlike anything he had hitherto experienced.

The flute player sat pondering in the darkness, trying to determine exactly why he was feeling so joyous after yesterday's spontaneous discourse with a traveling preacher. The teachings of Enoch had occupied his mind for the better part of the previous evening, only conceding focus to the preparations for travel he and his friend completed well after nightfall. It felt as if he were a new man, or at least on the way to becoming so, with a dramatic shift in his personal outlook. He was sure that he had never felt this inspired at any prior point in his life.

He was equally confident that his friend and host, Mahijah, sleeping peacefully just a few hands from him, felt the same way. How could he know this of the much older shepherd who had lead a very different life until they chanced upon each other a scant five months earlier? He knew it because of how they had discussed the preacher's discourse together. During their animated dialogue at the herdsman's tiny house—really no more than a stone shed—their eyes both shone with a new happiness, and their voices betrayed an eagerness for their trek. He could see it now in the faint traces of a smile on the grayed man's face, still lingering from yesterday.

Jubal caught his breath in a sudden epiphany. His mind had unexpectedly recovered a few experiences from his past—before becoming a rich and famous musician—that were equivalent to his current mood. He *had* previously felt something like this after all. While living within the walls of Haner, his gentle carpenter father of limited means would take him along with his mother and sisters to the harvest festival at the marketplace in the center of the city. Early in the morning, they would load his father's unsold wooden creations in the back of their mule cart, add the surplus of their foodstuffs, and head out on a day-long adventure. Jubal was just a child back then, but he remembered the excitement of traveling through the city, the harmony of being together with his family, and the glee at performing his original songs.

He also recalled the contentment and security of a full stomach from the seasonal spread—probably the most he would eat in one sitting the entire year—and the thrill of being asked by the passing crowds to play tunes from his flute for their amusement. His family would relax close at hand, cheering him along as they shared the remains of their feast and traded pieces of furniture from the cart with occasional shoppers. That was what he was feeling now, as he pondered his newest adventure, and he could wait no longer for it to begin.

"Awake, old man," the musician whispered gently, reaching over to his host with a less gentle nudge. "Awake. It is time for us to be off.

Remember what drives us, inspires us this morning. Zion awaits."

Mahijah was at first slow to respond to the prodding, still recovering from his night of little sleep, but then jolted upright as he grasped who was speaking to him. "Did you say *Zion?*" he queried anxiously, reaching back towards the musician for reassurance.

"Yes!" Jubal encouraged. "This dawn we set our feet on our declared journey towards Zion. The sun will soon be up, and your mule will need water and hay before we take our first steps. We will want full advantage of the desert morning's coolness."

Mahijah rubbed his eyes and sighed with deep relief, returning to the straw that was his own bed. "Good, good. Then yesterday, the sermon on the hill and the counsel of the seer, that was real enough? If so, all is well. Thoughts of Zion filled my dreams last night, and on awakening I feared it may have been nothing more than a strange hope. The *wild man*, his name was Enoch, if I am roused enough to remember correctly. Are we still resolved to pursue this fabled place? We have lost nothing so far, and may yet cancel our plans. We are free to choose, as I recall." Still reclining on one shoulder, a thin smile on his face, he glanced up to see the reaction of his young companion.

Jubal paused for a moment before recognizing the veiled jest in the herdsman's eyes, then chuckled as he rose from his warm, scratchy spot on the dirt floor. "Very funny, venerable one. You must be as eager for this journey as I am, though as the morning breaks it appears that I am far more alert than you. I have not forgotten our pledges. We are reborn this morning as free men. We both wish happiness, as everyone does. We are at liberty to make the choices that lead to it and accountable for those decisions. Such is our purpose, and we will not be deterred. So up, up I say! I will tend to the mule while you ready your shack for our absence."

Mahijah nodded in agreement as he finally rose from slumber. This was the most pleased he had felt in his nearly one hundred years of life. He looked around his rocky hut with its warm hearth and sturdy roof. He was grateful for those who had built it, the same who perished in the war with Heni just two years prior.

After many decades of sorrow—famine, betrayal, and toil to weary his very bones—he had removed himself from the land of Sharon for a new start, taking possession of this house so that he could raise sheep and sew spun cloth into cloaks. He became expert at both, but found more satisfaction in creating well-made and colorful robes for his customers. Neither wife nor children were alive to assist him or to give him comfort, but he befriended Jubal while selling his cloth in the market of Haner. They remained true to each other these last five months, sharing tales of their past grief and just yesterday leaning on each other to find something greater. The herdsman was glad to have such a friend as the musician, and expected they would ever be so, but his heart told him that he would never feel the warmth of his hut's hearth again. So be it. All was well.

With the house as secure as it could be made, and with the mule loaded with sacks of provisions, Mahijah's extra cloth, and his unsold cloaks, the friends started off on their six-day journey to the City of Zion, the sun just rising in the east. Their hearts were light and their minds full, only regretting that the kind tent-keeper who had shared his shade with them yesterday disappeared before they could tell him of their experience with the seer.

At that time, they had sat at the feet of Enoch, a prophet and leader in Zion, hearing from him how they could change their lives for the better and how his people were already striving to do so. They learned that the inhabitants of Zion formed a society of righteousness, full of joy despite their challenges, living in a place where their full potential was possible. The friends listened intently for the better part of the afternoon, unswayed by the unruly mob that yelled at and threatened to kill the wild man they claimed was come to defame and curse their proud city. The evangelist wanted to lead the two pilgrims to Zion himself, but could not ignore his previous obligations to preach in front of additional nations to the north. He instead revealed to them the route to Zion, and advised they travel to his city without him to see for themselves how its residents lived.

Last eventide, they had vowed to do just that.

Six days later, far along the route they had been shown, the artist and the cloak maker were still committed to their quest.

Despite Mahijah's advanced years, they had made decent time in following the directions Enoch had laid out for them. The route was not as obvious as they hoped, with at best a narrow, winding footpath to follow, but the instructions to head southward did not appear to have failed them. Though fatigued in body, their spirits refused to falter even when confronted with warnings from camel traders and spice haulers who crossed their path. Some merchants claimed the city was a myth, purely a cautionary tale to admonish children or entertain visitors and that the travelers would perish looking for it in vain. Others cautioned that the people of Zion were devils, barbarous savages who would tear them to pieces if they did not turn around and scurry back home.

If the friends harbored misgivings, they declined to give them a voice, remaining undeterred as the seventh day dawned. Having toiled these many days, they were determined to see their pilgrimage through to the end.

The morning was growing stale as the musician and the shepherd trudged over the crest of another sandy hill, the most recent of dozens that had crossed their shared path. But *this* hill was different, for as they peered over their veiled noses and through the tattered cloth protecting them from the constant, pelting sand, they abruptly stood fixed. Before them in the distance, shimmering in the permeating heat, was the object of their joint journey, and they paused in awe as they gazed upon it. Then, as if from an unseen signal, they sank as one to their knees.

"Zion!"

They exhaled the name simultaneously from their parched throats, a breathy release of equal parts elation and dread.

Elation, for this was their anticipated goal ever since leaving the suburbs of their homeland. What had once been only a hope and a promise appeared now to be a reality. Elation, because they had walked by faith to this point along their path, unfamiliar with the route leading to the city, trusting that it existed at all. Back in the land of Haner, stories of the city and its inhabitants were abundant, but legend and mystery had so exaggerated the tales as to make them all but implausible, and therefore mostly ignored. Few of the residents of Haner claimed any direct knowledge of Zion, and the second-hand rumors and wispy memories varied from one person to the next. A wizened merchant, bereft of former riches, whispered stories of gemmed walls and streets paved with gold. Inconceivable! A befuddled explorer, sitting in rags in the corners of the city, mumbled of angelic beings clothed in finery who feasted day and night on an endless supply of sumptuous meats, fruits, and grains. Outrageous! Who among them could be believed? And yet now before their eyes towered the promised city.

And dread, for if the city really existed, maybe the fearful stories were also true. For the first time on their journey, pernicious doubt clouded the minds of the travelers. Could Enoch have been a fraud, a liar whose actual aim was to send unwitting fools like themselves into the wilderness to die, slain like lambs to the slaughter by his evil cohorts? In their native land, equally nasty rumors spoke of terrible inhabitants in Zion, monsters who could command the very mountains to fall upon their enemies, or bid the rivers to drown their adversaries. A crippled soldier, disturbed by the memories of past battles, recounted odd tales of fighting an invisible enemy. Crazy talk! An aged orphan, begging for bread, recalled—for listeners willing to donate a fresh loaf—the horrors of wild animals driven to devour his kin. Dread, for the stories of dismay suddenly seemed the more powerful to the flute player and his shepherd.

The friends turned to look at each other, still on their knees, now clutching each other by the arms. With a few more hours of steady walking, they would stand before Zion's gate and know the truth of its mysteries for themselves.

"There it is!" yelled Jubal, his breathing heavy and fast. "After these many days, we have finally found it. And yet, I cannot move forward. My very core is seized with terror. I fear that I will not be able to rise to my feet and pass under the threshold of the city, but will die here in view of its doorstep."

Mahijah shared his friend's misgivings, but was not ready to succumb to them. Maybe his past troubles had better prepared him for this instant, or perhaps his advanced years had actually brought him the extra patience and wisdom folks tend to attribute to the aged. Or was it the simple stubbornness he learned from his sheep, an unwillingness to be forced along an alternate course.

"Remember the words of the prophet, and stand firm with me," he implored. "We are free to make our own decisions. Elect to push aside your fright, and in your choosing give me courage to do the same."

Jubal relaxed, almost embarrassed by his rash surrender compared to the humility, courage, and motivation of his more feeble friend. Obviously he could choose. He was his own agent, as are we all. Why should he give in to some ephemeral emotion such as fear? He need not panic. His course was as clear now as ever it had been, even more so with the finish in sight. Of course he would proceed, not because he was beholden to do so, but because such was his wish. The artist rose from his knees, his friend mimicking his example, and they strode forward to complete their journey to Zion.

Before long, the sand and stone covering the strait trail that had been their guide during most of their week-long passage turned into a compacted dirt road, showing signs of increased traffic. Grassy plains and trimmed pastures bordered the highway, with the impressive walls of Zion rising in front of them. Cattle lazily grazed on one side of the widening path, while sheep bleated from the other. An occasional, young herder could be seen leaning against an even more occasional tree, or practicing with a sling, or playing music on a lyre. Upon spying the friends in the road, the herdsmen would smile and wave, sometimes shout a brief greeting and then wait for some kind of reply before returning to their activities. Their salutations were welcoming, and each youth seemed cheerful, healthy, and at ease.

Presently, the road widened even more, enough to allow for two oxcarts traveling abreast. The dirt on its surface was replaced with some kind of clay and rock mixture and its edges were lined with low stones. Cultivated fields traded places with the former grasslands. The travelers recognized cucumbers, tomatoes, and date trees ripe with fruit sprouting from the ground nearby—all in tidy rows—but a short, bushy plant with yellow bulbs was a mystery to them. In the distance, they could clearly see wheat and corn waiving in a gentle breeze, and Jubal was certain that there were vineyards even further out.

By this time, solitary farmers and small groups of cultivators were visible across the countryside, busy at pruning or watering or weeding their crops. Older men, mature women, young girls and boys, and entire families seemed to be at work inspecting or picking produce. Carts were used to transport loads to waiting barns and silos. Other workers were seen making repairs to the buildings, or mending tools in the fields. Mahijah could detect no dwellings among the structures, which seemed odd to him, but Jubal did not appear to notice.

These field hands also hailed the travelers with smiles and friendly waves, making sure that they were acknowledged without interfering with whatever business the two might have. It was obvious to the musician and the shepherd that they were strangers in the land, but they did not feel themselves so. It was as if they were fellow citizens of the city whose return from some distant errand had been anticipated by their neighbors, who now showered them with welcoming calls as they walked by.

A deep voice from the east side of the road startled the pilgrims. A short, stocky man of maybe fifty years was reaping his adjacent field and had entered the road to offer his greeting. Hanging from his left arm was a wide basket half-full of dates. He extended his empty right hand, looking each of the friends directly in the eye before glancing down at the mule.

"Good morning! Now *there* is a tired beast if ever I saw one. I am Lamech, the son of my father by the same name. I do not think we have met before, but I am at your service. Are you visiting someone in Zion?"

Jubal was struck by the man's frank tone and lack of ceremony, which made him surprisingly approachable. He looked down at Lamech, but only because of his short frame. The stranger was good-natured, polite, and truly squat in height. From under a wide-brimmed hat, he wore a full head of black hair, with an equally full and dark beard running down his face. His home-made clothing was plain and consisted of light colors, no doubt to counter the heat of the sun. His feet were bare and covered in soil. With a professional eye, Mahijah admired the quality of this stranger's covering, observing the unusually elegant apparel being worn for such menial fieldwork. Both travelers recognized the look of Enoch in the diminutive man's face. It was less a familial similarity than a familiar glow, but surely even that could only be an odd coincidence.

Jubal spoke for the two of them while Mahijah allowed his pack animal to feed on some grass to the side of the road, for there were no stray blades of green to be seen on the trail itself. "I am Jubal, a flutist from Haner, and this is my friend Mahijah, a herdsman and cloak maker of Sharon, recently moved to my country. We are strangers to Zion, but not to your leader, Enoch. We have sat at his feet, listened to his preaching, and have been sent by him to see your city for ourselves. He promised it to be a land of peace and prosperity where we could find happiness."

The artist was surprised at how natural it was to speak with Lamech. They had barely encountered each other, and already Jubal felt comfortable telling him his personal history. He suspected that he would divulge to this humble farmer anything the man might ask.

"Then we are well met, my new friends," said the dark farmer. "Please, allow me to call you *friends*. Enoch is well-known to our people, for we owe much of what we have accomplished to him. If my wits are not diminished, your expedition from Haner will have taken you just over six days. You must be exhausted. Come, join me in the shade for a while and relax. You can help me assess the ripeness of my crop. You will easily make the city before nightfall. Leave your animal on the side of the road with its grass; it will come to no harm. These roads are the safest in the whole region."

The three of them walked off the road and through several rows of mature trees, Mahijah wondering what fruit or vegetable awaited their taste-testing in the shade.

Jubal deliberated on how Enoch, the missionary who claimed to be the poorest man in all of Zion, could be famed among its occupants and still be impoverished. All the worldly rulers he had ever known were wealthy, owning fine linen, lavish tables, and coffers full of silver and gold, elevated to high status because of those very coffers. But this nomadic leader and teacher had claimed to be the *poorest* man in Zion. The musician felt the need to solve this mystery before too long.

Jubal decided to set his irritating thought aside for the present as they passed through the final row of trees. In doing so, they were surprised to see a modest woman and a lively band of children sitting together in a large, rough circle, their own date baskets resting amongst them in the soil. The eldest of the children could not have been more than twenty years of age. Upon noticing the trio, everyone in the large group hailed them with happy voices, gesturing for them to come sit with the family in the shade.

"Friends, this is my wife, Zillah, and most of our children," said Lamech, introducing his cherished spouse and their enthusiastic offspring. "Family, these are my new friends from the land of Haner who have come to visit our city. I have invited them to sample our dates with us."

Zillah smiled warmly, keeping her seat on the ground and extending her hand in greeting. The children all rose and approached the travelers, some extending a hand, others offering a hug, all speaking happy words of welcome. The oldest of the youngsters knew of Haner and made casual comments about its agriculture, its demographics, and its recent war with Heni. The younger girls and boys asked after any family or hobbies their visitors might have, setting them at ease with their innocent and animated exchange.

Sensing a natural lull in the pleasantries, Lamech interrupted with a request and a question, saying to the guests, "Please have a seat and taste our dates. Are they large and sweet enough to your liking, or should we allow them to ripen a few days more before harvesting?"

Several of the younger children led Jubal and Mahijah to sit next to them on the warm ground, pulling them close and immediately telling the strangers everything that rose to the top of their young minds. The duo were instantly restful among the family, astonished at how swiftly and intuitively they had been gathered in between them. Lamech sent one of the older sons from the circle to water Mahijah's mule, allowing his visitors to relax and enjoy their company. Following Zillah's example, they started to pull fruit from nearby baskets to taste. They were delicious! After some tranquil conversation, plenty of juicy nourishment, and revitalizing, cool water to drink, Mahijah spoke to the father, having a professional question on his mind.

"We thank you for such a warm welcome. Your family is a refreshing breeze, and the dates are plump and tasty—the sweetest I have savored. We must have interrupted your work in the fields. Do your wife and children always help with your harvesting? I have seen older boys assisting their fathers in such a manner, plowing and sowing as well, but never the girls or younger children. Your youngsters speak as if they are well-educated. They must be missing their schooling while in the fields."

There were few topics Lamech enjoyed discussing more than his family and his work, so he was eager to give a thorough response. "We are glad you have come to Zion to learn something of our city and its inhabitants. We must visit with you again over the course of your stay, hoping it will be as lengthy as you can spare. Already, you may have noticed differences in our land from your own. You are correct that Zillah does not always join me in the fields with the children, but we make sure that the family is involved in all aspects of our work—to the degree that we can. Cultivating is not my effort alone, as you alluded to in your question, but our trade together. We support each other as we toil in the soil, learning the various tasks and helping as our abilities allow. The same goes for helping the children in their studies, whether it be languages or history or mechanics. For this is our cooperative work to do, and we are motivated to make it successful."

"Yours is truly an odd arrangement, but not without its merits, I suppose," the shepherd continued with a follow-up question as the artist reclined in the shade. "Do all farming families in Zion arrange their daily chores as you do?"

Zion was another of Lamech's favorite conversational themes, so his guests were in for a treat. "There is a lot of agreement among families within our community, especially on the most important of our societal affairs. However, the details of how to perform our labors is something that each individual—each couple or family—is free to decide for herself. Zillah and I prefer to work together as much as possible. It reminds us of our shared purpose: to work as one for our collective success. Yes, there are neighbors of ours who take the same approach, specifically one who is using our exact methodology as his model, but many others find a different way. It is actually valuable that we each attack our responsibilities with varying techniques so that we might learn improvements from each other. Our family cannot claim credit for being the first to work in the fields in this manner."

The pilgrims remembered what Enoch had taught them of freedom, responsibility, and choices, but they were content to listen and partake of their succulent snack, so the farmer continued.

"Once we had decided to marry, Zillah and I discussed at length what we were going to pursue as our combined purpose, what would motivate our efforts as husband and wife. We wanted to be knit together in a unified vision for becoming happy, as our parents before us had been, even if it were to change a little over the decades.

"Then, when we married and formally became one, we discussed more specifically how to best organize our new household and came to some initial conclusions. Ever since, it has always been our practice to figure things out in our minds together, considering options before reaching agreement on actions. Having a cohesive direction is selfless by its very nature, as participants in the vision need to sacrifice some of their personal egoism to attain any combined intent.

"After our third child was born, we heard friends talking about how farming together had benefited their children, so we decided to try it out. We have since found that when we work the earth jointly, our hearts and the hearts of our children are more closely intertwined. It is a concrete exposition of our shared ambition in life. Purpose unifies people."

"Plus, there is nothing we cannot overcome when we cooperate in this fashion," Zillah added, confirming her husband's message for the pilgrims. "Records kept for hundreds of years by farming families throughout our land validate our modern methods. Output has steadily increased, while the amount of required physical activity has either remained constant or decreased over time."

"And look!" she exclaimed, her face beaming as she spied her boy coming back from the road. "The prodigal son has returned at last."

Lamech's son rejoined the group, having supplied the cloak maker's mule with all it could drink. After giving him a chance to grab some more dates and draughts of water, the farmer stood to mark the end of their mid-day break and the need to get back to their harvesting.

"Speaking of work," he pivoted the conversation, "would you like to see first-hand how we reap our dates? I am sure we have extra baskets. We intend to complete six more rows before the day is done."

The children jumped up to return to their labors, shouting with delight at the prospect of their new friends joining them. Jubal and Mahijah were more than rested by now and were excited to assist their kind hosts. They had consumed plenty of dates and cool water, but felt neither guilt nor shame at taking the food that was so freely given. In addition to being curious, they truly felt included as part of the family—like distant uncles, perhaps—and wanted to contribute to its success.

Thanks to help from its adopted uncles, the day of gathering ended sooner than expected for Lamech's family. *Too soon* the two of them thought, as they had thoroughly enjoyed their experience, even while covered in sweat and tired from their exertions. Lamech had devoted substantial time to methodically explain his special harvesting process to the travelers. Firstly, he thanked them by name for being willing to help. Secondly, he clarified for them why it was important to finish the remaining rows. Thirdly, he pointed out the exact portion of the picking that they would handle, and then fourthly—finally—he meticulously demonstrated how it was to be done. It was an education neither of the uncles had expected, but they reacted with humble gratitude. What better way to learn of Zion than to participate in all its activities, even work?

The sun was lowering but still bright as the entire company, a productive day of work behind them, gathered their fruits and tools and walked towards their house located within the northern wall of the city, the shepherd's mule in tow. This concept of urban living for field workers was another novelty for the uncles to absorb, for they were accustomed to farmers and cattlemen living outside the city in the meadowed suburbs close to their employment. Lamech explained that all of his neighbors lived within the city walls, including shepherds, goat herders, wine growers, and those of similar occupations alike. The practice resulted in amplified safety for the occupants of the land. This was a significant benefit because every life—every soul—was precious in and of itself. Zion wept when any were lost. But security was only a secondary advantage.

The primary reason for this tradition—a loftier reason—was so that everyone could participate in the life of the city and its common purpose. The motivation for individual contentment was magnified when combined with others of a similar mind. Striving to become a happy people was a cohesive aspiration, best expressed and remembered when everyone was present. At a high level, the residents of Zion were united in their drive and desire. They were of one heart and one mind.

As the successful harvesters reached the center of the three northern entrances to the city, the two aliens stopped in their tracks to gaze at the large opening in the even larger walls. Jewels of different colors and sizes decorated the arch above the opening, sparkling in the dimming sunlight. Engraved into the base of the walls, adjacent to the entryway, were names the pair did not recognize, but that obviously had required great skill to carve.

The gate itself rested wide open on three massive hinges, attached to the wall on one side. It was different from every other gateway the travelers had witnessed. It was constructed of what looked like a dull, silvery frame with a circular white sphere suspended in the center, bulging outward from its metal moorings. On the visible surface of the opaque door were intricate and inspiring etchings that appeared to jump off its curved face and into the wide world surrounding it. On the west side of the pearly ball was engraved a tree in full bloom, leaves large and reaching upward, branches laden with their plump goodness. On the east side were etched the images of a man and a woman, hand in hand and clothed in sheepskin, fleeing from the tree while gazing with longing behind them.

Seeing that the visitors had halted and were engrossed with the beauty of the entryway, Lamech motioned for Zillah to go ahead with the children, indicating that he would follow a little later. She beamed with a knowing grin, hurrying her progeny along through the entrance. Watchmen, standing on the towers above and on the ground to either side of the gate, noticed the amazement of the pilgrims and seemed to chuckle at the familiar spectacle before losing interest. One waved to Lamech with a smile, obviously an associate of some kind, but felt no need to approach.

"Spectacular!" Jubal shouted, unable to restrain his admiration and praise for the magnificence in open view. "The stories are true, at least those regarding the splendor of your city. Anyone can plainly see from its entrance and walls alone—its towers, domes, and spires rising above in the distance—that there is much wealth and security to be found inside."

His shepherding friend was equally amazed, standing in reverence before the immense snowy door, his hand loosely holding the rope that lazily fell from the head of his beast.

"Yes, I suppose it is true," Lamech conceded. "We risk underappreciating beautiful things if we do not take time to notice them. It is definitely a pleasing place to live. I think we have become one. Now, are you expecting to enter the city for the evening, or to pitch your tent outside? We would be most pleased for you to join us at our residence, but we do not want to impose." Lamech was accustomed to the glory of the city, though he was reminded of it more clearly whenever someone in his company beheld it for the first time. He was more interested in the welfare of his guests.

"Impose? We are the ones who have already imposed upon you. We are indeed grateful for your sincere invitation, but with so many offspring your abode must already be bursting at its seams. Would you even have room for two visitors?" Mahijah looked down at his mule and sighed. "I mean *three* visitors?"

"Of course, of course. We always have room in our house for uncles … and their pets. Besides, the children would be disappointed if you did not favor them with your company again. Moreover, I wager Zillah will have a hearty meal waiting for us. Come and see."

Lamech did not wait for a reaction, but gently grabbed the mule from its owner, taking the lead rope and mildly slapping it against the animal's hindquarters, guiding his guests under the threshold and through the door of the city.

The travelers walked unhurriedly, letting their eyes and ears wander, attempting to take in the whole spectacle of the city. The streets inside Zion were not at all what they anticipated. The avenues were wide and level, overlaid with the same strange mixture as the road outside the walls though made of a much finer and smoother blend. They bulged slightly towards the center, with gutters on either side apparently designed to catch excess rainfall.

Aside from their construction, the larger wonder was that the streets bustled with activity at this late hour. Scattered shops were starting to close as the sunset approached, but the boulevards were still full of motion. Torches, positioned at regular intervals along the walls and buildings lining the lanes, were being lit in advance of the darkness. Adults and children continued to socialize and play all about them. It was as if an intermission were ending and the third act of a stirring and familiar play was forthcoming. Every person they noticed was involved in some deed designed to prepare for the next scene, and, though not clearly coordinated, each of their actions seemed relevant. They all added something inimitable to the readiness.

The diversity in the streets was unexpected, though everyone was courteous and respectful in their manners. Men, women, and children of all ages were present. They wore clothing of all styles and fashions, most of which Mahijah had never dreamed of seeing before. And while the colors and patterns appeared to vary sharply from one person to the next, they were alike in that nothing was pretentious or gaudy, nothing distinguished an upper class of people from anything lower.

"This is an incredible sight for us to see. What is happening?" asked Jubal. He and the cloak maker were both acquainted with the streets within large cities, but this was unusual, impressive. They wondered if their amazement would find an end before they rested for the night.

"Let me think," Lamech tried to respond, tapping his chin with his finger and furrowing his brow in thought. "Tonight is the first day of the week, so … honestly I am not sure. It could be a musical concert, or a discussion on our building plans for next season. Maybe an open house for the new sculptures that have just been completed, or a lecture on gardening techniques. I *do* know there are games with neighbors every third night in seven, something I always look forward to and enjoy. Four evenings from now is a poetry reading—my daughter will be presenting one of her originals. There is always something going on, chances to interact with each other, share our skills and talents, or to just relax and chat. Oh look, here is my friend, Japheth. I must say *hello*."

The farmer took a few minutes to speak with his friend of many years, at the same time introducing to him the travelers—as he had to his own family—and inviting them to join in their exchange. Once finished chatting, they continued their walk. Lamech was repeatedly stopped and greeted by additional friends and acquaintances as he led his visitors through the streets. On each occurrence, he introduced the flute player and the cloak maker to his neighbors—short and tall, timid and outgoing, in a hurry or content to linger. Regardless of who they met, analogous conversations ensued, though they were peculiar in their particulars. Every welcoming encounter was a treat.

Those who paused to hail the trio all spoke the same language, but the travelers could hear unique accents peppering their speech. It was evident from the shades of the faces they met—ranging from deepest black to palest white—that this nation had formed from a mixture of ancestral backgrounds. But nobody, except for the newcomers, seemed to care about or even notice the assortment on display. From Lamech's account of oneness, the pilgrims had expected the residents of Zion to be mostly uniform, similar to each other in skin color, mannerisms, activities, and dress. What they saw was the opposite of their assumption.

Mahijah voiced their mutual observation, stating, "Everyone is so different. We have never experienced such a variety of people in one location, nor in multiple locations for that matter. I thought you told us that Zion was *one*?"

"What I told you is true. We are one, where it counts the most," Lamech chuckled softly. "The things we own, like the clothing and animals and carts you see, are personal preferences serving as outward statements of our tastes and inclinations. Our peculiar histories, our likes and dislikes, and our skin color are all part of who we are individually. We work all kinds of trades, creating new ones to fill unpredicted needs as they arise. We study different topics and engage in divergent leisure activities. We are each unique, and we recognize and learn from—even celebrate—our contrasts.

"Speak to any of our men or women and you will find that they are yet more distinctive in their thoughts and opinions, their ideas of how to solve a problem, and their methods for expressing those designs. But we are the same—nearly identical—in our commitment to each other: our cooperative desire to achieve happiness. We mourn together when gloomy, rejoice together when blissful, and always love and assist one another. Our end mission is the same, despite individual efforts as singular as every one of us. This oneness is among our stoutest strengths, and the drive behind our burgeoning success. We live to serve."

The herdsman considered the farmer's words. He figured there must be great power in combined ambition. How would his life have differed for the better if he had been of one heart and one mind with his father, or with his demanding wife? What would have become of the couple who sheltered him in his youth, if only they had found a way to share in the inspiration of their adventurous daughter? Come to think of it, nothing short of the jubilant vision he shared with his companion could have pulled him, at his advanced age, through the desert and safely inside the boundaries of this incredible nation. He was still processing this realization when his musical friend chimed in on a separate observation.

"Since entering the city, I have not seen any soldiers," noted Jubal. "Nor, for that matter, have I observed any beggars or pickpockets in your streets, no drunkards or dubious characters to dampen the mood. We meet more than our fill of all those types in Haner. Is there no strife nor crime within your city?"

"It does warm one's heart, does it not?" the farmer agreed, tapping his chest as he adjusted his grip on the mule's rope. "We do not find that sort of activity much at all any more, though it was not always so. In the beginning, there was a lot more conflict, though even then it was milder than you probably imagine. It is fascinating to compare archives from those days with our current chronicles. Persons acting in the manner you described tended to feel uninspired by our image for the future, excluded from it for one reason or another. Since it is easier to reach an end that is clearly articulated, we helped them feel more integrated with the rest of the community, persuaded them that they were vital to our eventual triumph, and opened their eyes to what we could achieve together. The situation has been getting better ever since, especially in the last few years. We really feel united in our expectations."

"This is incredible to witness! What power there must be in having a shared vision, that such a possession can set a course for behavior, maybe change a person's nature?" Jubal turned as he spoke, facing the others and blocking their progress along the street. He was so eager to understand the customs of this people that he needed to pause and focus. "But victory depends on more than a communal dream. How do the inhabitants of Zion coordinate among themselves, plan for their common futures, and determine when their efforts have been fruitful? What do you—"

Lamech interrupted the musician. They had been making steady progress towards the farmer's house and were now nearing its front door. "Jubal, I see that you and Mahijah may have more to ask of me, but I am famished after our day working in the fields, and Zillah must be wondering what keeps us from home. May we continue to the house for some hot soup and roasted rabbit? I promise that I will then do my best to respond to any more questions."

Their new brother had been so agreeable in assisting them that the uncles had forgotten he had a family waiting for him. For their part, they had been so keen to learn about the occupants of Zion that they had also failed to notice their own bellies were impatient to be filled. Plus, the mule would be wanting some nourishment for itself. It seemed that everyone in the party was hungry! They readily consented to finish walking to the house and formed a rank of three abreast for the final stretch.

It was in that moment that Jubal fully understood the great truth he had heard, but not truly grasped, since first meeting Lamech. The farmer, the musician, and the shepherd were as different as any three people to be found on these streets tonight, but they were united in their purpose to eat a warm meal. Their solidarity was unquestionable. In this matter, at least, they were one.

MUTUAL VISION UNITES PEOPLE

4

Dwelt in Righteousness

Jubal was perplexed as he struggled to reconcile the events of the last seven days. Barely a week ago, he had languished as a despairing pauper in the once-great city of Haner, at the mercy of thieves and enemy soldiers, with only his custom-made flute to remind him of his happier childhood. Tonight, he walked through the fabled streets of the mightiest city in legend, undoubtedly a nation more glorious and accommodating than any he had experienced in his admittedly short reality. He was a protected guest in Zion, with a full stomach, loyal friends, and a shared vision of future happiness. The reversal of his circumstances seemed too good to be true.

Not too long ago, his talent and fame as a musician had filled his purse with silver and gold. But his riches, instead of contributing to a life of stability and peace, brought him only uncertainty and heartache. The promise of a loving marriage precipitously grew cold, and the beauty and innocence of his music were replaced with greed and cynicism. With alarming alacrity, the army of a rival city, led by a more powerful king—a more violent king—attacked the age-old land of Haner, breached its walls, and enslaved its occupants. In the horrific aftermath of the invasion, when he discovered his father's family killed and his estranged wife missing, his heart broke and he slumped into misery.

It was the war that had made a final end of him—or so he thought. Of a truth he was still poor, with only the clothes on his back and his pan flute of nine pipes to his name. But he *did* have a close friend, Mahijah, the thin, gray shepherd of the land of Sharon who had accompanied him on their trek. It was thanks to the shepherd that he was even here in the first place. And he *was* happy in the City of Holiness, with a joy that the glory of all his former wealth could not match.

Yes, the war had knocked him down, but it had not finished him. There was hope for him yet.

So too was there hope for his dear traveling companion. Like the flute player, Mahijah had been no stranger to sorrow, experiencing personal tragedies to equal that of his friend. His mother died in labor giving him life, and his father and older siblings all blamed him for her loss. Abandoned as a youth, he worked as an only child in the house of an older couple until famine took them. A loveless marriage endured not many years before another food shortage took the life of his wife and children. He did develop an extraordinary talent as a herdsman and sewer of cloaks, but was never able to monetize it while in his homeland. On the edge of physical survival and approaching his emotional limits, he transplanted himself to war-ravaged Haner in anticipation of acquiring a small parcel of land and a tiny flock of sheep.

Devastated by decades of ruin, the shepherd imagined being alone the rest of his life, until his fortune changed and he happened across Jubal in the streets of his new city. The older man was able to sway the younger into relating his grief-stricken life story, and to listen in turn to his own sad tale. A new friendship formed, and Mahijah, weary of the wickedness of the world, decided to fight in favor of its success. With his naturally cheerful company, he started to turn Jubal away from anguish. Then, just seven days ago, he convinced the musician to join him in heeding the advice of an itinerant preacher outside their city.

Jubal persisted in poverty, but now he was no longer despairing, for who among us can continue in sadness with a caring friend by our side and a joyous purpose in life?

The new hope the musician felt had started to rise in his breast the day he turned away from the marketplace to investigate the words of a stranger. From the gentle westerly slope outside of Haner, Enoch, the prophet, spoke of happiness and freedom and recommended the two friends make a journey to seek after both. They arrived in the land of Zion just that morning and met their current host and his family farming in the fields without its walls. Lamech, husband and father to a formidable pack of offspring, greeted them like brothers as they approached. He welcomed their tired limbs, fed their empty bellies, and invited them to stay the night at his house inside the city walls.

At present, they were following the farmer to his abode in Zion, slowly walking through the streets of Enoch's city, the shepherd's mule plodding behind them on its rope. Even after a full day of travel and new experiences, the friends were not tired. They had learned so much from Lamech that they should have expected to be overwhelmed, but the opposite was the case. Their intellectual and emotional appetites had expanded to match that of their bodies. They were still hungry, unready for the day to end, but they did have Lamech's pledge that, once a hot meal and a short rest were behind them, he would fully entertain any further question they might pose. Jubal intended to hold him to that strategy.

Meanwhile, the two travelers continued to admire the streets of Zion and its occupants. Like Lamech, the lanes were as modest and unassuming as they were vibrant and refined. Lit with bright torches, they were clean, tidy, and wide enough to accommodate large groups of pedestrians comfortably. No dust rose to choke travelers, for the pathways were covered in a hardened paste that made walking smooth and clean. The passersby in the lanes—young and old, tall and short—all exuded merriness, speaking enthusiastically and laughing out loud with each other. The cheerfulness and kindness in their conversation was comforting.

They were all engaged in some activity or another: moving covered stones into positions along the way, hanging comely charcoal sketches between murals carved on the walls, arranging benches in key locations. Youths kicked a ball, maneuvering through the more leisurely and elderly walkers, sometimes being joined by the more adventurous among them. Pretense and pride played no part in their midst, for though their clothing was colorful and of a high quality, such was true for all. Just as Lamech had been assuring and welcoming, the visiting friends were convinced that they would have received a similar reception from anyone who may have first greeted them to this land.

The three men continued walking—the sun already set—until they approached a large but unassuming house towards the middle of the city. As they arrived, the same son who had watered Mahijah's mule earlier that afternoon exited the house, taking it from his father without a grumble and leading it around a corner to their barn.

Lamech preceded his new friends through the front door of the house. It was to them a replica of the city itself, clean and humble in its magnificence. Shining candles were abundant, making the residence cheery and bright while allowing the family to finish their daily tasks. By its size alone one might have thought a prince lived within. Bedrooms were plenteous, many with private hearths for fires. The spacious kitchen, with its utilitarian cooking coals, assorted pots, and related tools, included a cozy area for the children to play. An adjacent courtyard opened to the night sky, offering a gorgeous view of stars, but was currently covered by a shiny blue cloth designed to protect its occupants from rain. The household furnishings were suitably plentiful and more practical than lavish, exhibiting an abundance without excess.

Lamech guided his guests into the main room, removing his brimmed hat and stroking his black beard. A low table rested in the center of the room, with plenty of cushions surrounding it. As they entered, the patriarch's children were just clearing the remains of their evening meal—chiefly rabbit and a soup of legumes from the look of it. Happy to see each of them again, they ran over to their father and adopted uncles before being shooed out of the room by Zillah, their mother. The uncles were reminded of Lamech's large family and concluded that the size of his house had been planned in proportion to the size of his responsibility.

"Here you are," Lamech's wife declared, not surprised in the least that her husband had convinced the travelers to join them for the evening. "Please do come sit down and eat. We have plenty to spare."

Zillah was the model of patience and serenity. The peace of her visage was reflected in the house and its occupants. There was no fighting or evil speaking to be witnessed, no vulgar language or mean confrontation. Like the streets outside its front door, a spirit of charity naturally pervaded the lodging. It was a most welcome environment, one that the uncles had not been privileged to experience in their own lands.

Zillah left the room briefly, returning with what was to the two friends nothing short of a festival feast: trays carrying abundant meats and legume soup—as they had previously seen—but also bearing fruits, breads, cheese, and wine for their enjoyment. Two of her boys helped haul in the repast, innocently displaying the respect and politeness that their new uncles had so quickly grown to expect, and which their father had learned long ago to appreciate.

And feast the men did. Hungry after a day of toil, travel, and discussion, all three dove into the meal with well-mannered abandon. The uncles recognized all of the various dishes, common as they were throughout the region, but were pleasantly surprised by their extraordinary tastiness. Perhaps they *were* in the palace of a prince! The flavor of the food was as satisfying as its measure.

They ate until their stomachs would permit no more, then lounged on the cushions while two of Lamech's girls cleared the table, leaving a pitcher of water and a bowl of dates for the men. As the three sat in silence, the girls made a quiet return to a small fireplace at the far end of the room, one of them strumming lightly and skillfully on a lyre, the other intently reading from a book of loosely-bound pieces of parchment. The warmth of the building, the muted happy sounds here and there, and the fullness of their bellies were soothing to such a degree that the men started drifting asleep. When the lady of the house returned to stand by the table, her gentle voice aroused them from their reveries.

"I hope each of you has reached his fill. Lamech, my love, I am off to sleep. Remember, we have more rows to harvest in the morning, and Cain—our eldest son," the aside being for the benefit of her guests, "is due to join us in the fields. His wife might assist as well, if she feels up to it in her condition. Jubal and Mahijah, your room is prepared when you are ready to retire. Please make yourselves at home with us for as long as you like, though do remember there are children already slumbering."

Her authentic smile and willing tone presented nobody reason to question her sincerity. She gave the newcomers a wave of her hand and wished all the men a *goodnight.*

"My dear, you have taught our children well," Lamech complimented his spouse, rising and giving her an embrace before she could leave the room. "I am as fortunate a man as any in Zion. Rest yourself until the morning. I will replace the candles and see the older girls to bed, joining you before too long. But first, I suspect our brothers have more questions to ask of me, now that you have spoiled them with the succulence of our table."

The uncles thanked their departing hostess for as delicious a meal as they had ever enjoyed, and they all bade her a *goodnight* in return.

Lamech was correct. With their physical hunger satiated, the uncles were reminded of their thirst to discover lasting happiness. Enoch had promised the friends that they could find it in Zion, teaching them while atop the mount outside of Haner that happiness comes from exercising freedom to make good choices. He pointed them on their southward journey a week ago.

The farmer had received them in his fields earlier this very day. He taught them how inspiring expectations were vital to realizing goals, especially for a single-minded society, and the travelers were eager to hear what more Lamech could tell them along those lines.

Jubal wasted no time in speaking up, the soft strains of the lyre on the other side of the room providing a soothing backdrop to their conversation. "As you remember from our earlier exchanges, our homeland of Haner was not a place of comfort for me. Frankly, I was in the depths of despair, with only the occasional buttressing from my longsuffering friend here to pull my head above water. I led a miserable existence, and the herdsman was not much better off."

Jubal glanced towards his companion, who closed his eyes with a confirming nod of his head. He continued.

"The first day of last week, by some unexpected, favorable twist of fate, we had both determined that we would put our sadness behind us and seek counsel from selected residents in our nation who could teach us how to be cheerful for once and for all. Above all else, we wanted to be perpetually happy, and would not be dissuaded from it. At that very moment—by some miracle—we heard that your king, Enoch, was preaching outside our city gate, and were persuaded that he would guide us to our goal. We found him on the hill, and he taught us that all people were destined to find happiness, if they would but choose to seek it.

"Freedom, he explained, was the foundation upon which our choices rested, and we comprehended his words as much as novice pupils could. Today, through the grace of you and your family, we have been the beneficiaries of the service and love you claimed motivates the inhabitants of Zion. We have clearly seen the unity within your own household, and how this oneness in heart and mind is duplicated throughout the streets of your city. My question is this: what do you do as a people to achieve your vision?"

Lamech leaned backward a bit, taking in the musician's inquiry with a deep exhale before calmly replying.

"Enoch is truly a leader in our city," he conceded, "but we have no king except our God. The seer himself will tell you the same. He is a great teacher, but not the source of the knowledge. Zion has but *one* King."

"Pardon me, my friend. I intended no affront," Jubal stammered, worried that he had inadvertently offended his dear host. But he saw only benevolence in Lamech's face, without a trace of hurt.

Mahijah, older and wiser than the young musician, grinned and bowed his head, confident that there was no malice in their host's retort. He knew they were in the hands of a brother, a trusted friend who only wished them well. He considered himself ready to accept whatever the squat, black-bearded farmer might tell them.

"You will need to try much harder than *that* to injure my feelings!" Lamech chortled casually as he had earlier in the day. "If there was ever an offense, all is forgiven. Give it no more thought. Rather, let me address your question. In the City of Enoch, we all share a vision of love and service, striving to secure our own happiness by stimulating it in others. This is what motivates us, prompting us to take moral and virtuous actions in line with that vision. Our collective aim is all the brighter and stronger for having the support of so many others seeking the same."

"Yes, we have seen that," said the herdsman. He was more eager than impatient, but sometimes it was hard to distinguish one emotion from the other. "Without mentioning it specifically, we could tell from your neighbors that you were all unified in purpose. It was obvious from a distance. But what do you do to achieve that end?"

Lamech loved speaking about Zion, its precepts and blessings. He was just a farmer, no more informed nor capable than any of his neighbors. However, in this land there was no such thing as *just* or *only* when it came to people. Everyone was equally valuable and alike in their passion for their cause. He advanced the sermon already in progress.

"Our ripe dates which you tasted this afternoon, they did not spring magically from the ground, but were the result of much effort. That effort started when I became a farmer. I could have worked stone, or composed poetry, or raised cattle—any number of professions to earn my keep—but I chose to cultivate the land. That is now a part of who I am. I suppose I could change my profession, but I enjoy the challenge and marvel of it, so I remain an agrarian.

"As such, I support my own life and those of my household by contributing to the welfare of the larger community within which I dwell. My desire is to grow healthy, sumptuous crops for my family to eat and for me to sell in the market. In this way, I serve the people around me. I have a passion for becoming one of the best cultivators of dates in the land, and I toil six days a week to realize my vision. But prior to first burdening my oxen with a plow, and before placing my first seed in the soil, I created a plan of what I needed to do to be successful. I determined in my mind where and when to sow, how to organize my fields, and who I would hire to labor alongside me. I set goals for how much to grow and when to harvest. I devoted much time and effort to study and calculations—conscious thought—and only then, with my stratagem in place, did I begin the physical labor to achieve my mental conception.

"In due course, Zillah became my wife, and began helping me with the planning. So involved does she prefer to be in our work that often it is more accurate to say that *I* help *her*. Our marriage has significantly changed my previous approach to cultivating our land. Despite our best efforts, we frequently need to adjust our plans to take advantage of opportunities or to recover from unforeseen obstacles. Sick oxen or a dry season may force us to update our goals, but it is these goals that give structure to our pursuit. They plainly outline what we must do for me to become the exceptional agriculturalist we know I can be.

"In general, this is what we do to achieve our happiness. We devise a strategy with goals designed to lead us to the desired end, and then we relentlessly pursue them. As brothers and sisters in Zion, we take the same approach. We must together have aims and objectives that provide a path for our shared vision. What actions are we to take to show love for each other? What can and should we do to serve the neighbors around us? What is the blueprint for Zion?"

Lamech paused to sip water from his cup, giving his eager listeners a chance to absorb what he had described so far. They said nothing at first, intently waiting for him to answer his own question. But when wisdom was slow to arrive, eagerness overcame patience once more.

"*Well*," blurted Mahijah. "What *is* the blueprint you follow to become united and happy?"

"It is simply this: we live by every word that proceeds from the mouth of God." The farmer was happy to indulge them as best he could, but of a sudden, his audience became less certain, shifting in their seats.

Lamech forged ahead to ease their discomfort. "Through his mouthpieces, our Creator teaches us how to behave with love and in service towards each other. This is our path to happiness. Enoch, our guide, the kindly wild man who visited your homeland seven days ago, is one of those oracles. The wise sayings you heard from his mouth came first from the mouth of God and are the same preachings we accept in Zion. Enoch keeps a book received from his fathers, mouthpieces like him. It is a collection of these instructions bound together where they can be remembered and added to from time to time as God pleases. Our seer safeguards the original, but scribes make copies for us to have in our congregations and families so that the words can ever be before us. Our family has one here in this room, laying on that stand between the windows over there."

The visitors followed Lamech's hand as he gestured towards the wall across from the table where they sat. They had not noticed the narrow, mostly vertical wooden stand until now, it fitting naturally into the furnishings of the chamber. He nodded to answer Mahijah's silent question, inviting the shepherd to retrieve the book resting on the top, slanted shelf and bring it back to the table. He did so, opening it on the smooth, wooden planks so that his companion could view it beside him.

It was an unusual instrument for the era, never seen before by either of the guests. Between two small, thin squares of wood were sheets of parchment, carefully sewn with strong threads to each other and to the wooden covers, holes having been punched as pathways for the strings.

As astounded as the guests were to see the book, they were more interested in its contents. Ornate writing in clean, black strokes, attractive to the eye yet straightforward to read, covered the bulk of the pages. The language was that of their native tongue, written in traditional format but easy for them to comprehend. They immediately noticed familiar phrases as they flipped through the pages, passages they had heard on the hill of Haner as they listened to the evangelist barely a week ago. More reading revealed similar sermons on various topics, all relating to the same core principles. Reaching about a third of the volume's thickness from the front cover, the writing ended and was replaced by blank sheets. Behind the last page, a stack of loose pages in several different hands had been carefully inserted. The uncles flipped back to the beginning of the book, taking turns leafing through its contents.

Lamech picked up his tutoring from where he had left it,

anticipating his guests' concerns and questions. "It is by walking in harmony with these commands—first delivered by venerable Adam—that we are assured to one day reach the glorious future we all desire. As we are true to these principles, we dwell in righteousness and prove our devotion for our Maker. Primary among them is to love each other. The empty pages are for future insights that Enoch or other seers will convey. As new messages are received, we employ scribes to update the book with the most recent lectures.

"The loose pages are letters from my parents and grandparents, words of counsel they were inspired to share with me, which I share with Zillah and the children. Periodically, we will add them to a second book, kept on a lower shelf of the same stand containing a history of our family and important secular events of our day. Most if not all families keep this separate journal as well, providing numerous independent accounts to verify the facts of our societal past. With such a widely distributed and redundant library within our society, it is much more difficult for us to be deceived. For myself, I impart my own divine dreams to my family, writing to my son Cain so that he might have heaven's guidance preserved in a family journal of his own. God speaks as often as there are ears to listen. His wish is that we would all be prophets."

"But the gods do not rule among men! They are symbols, figures, miniature statues who love ceremony and remaining uninvolved in the comings and goings of those they torment. It is their *priests* who insist on interfering with our lives, demanding more and more tribute, eating our fine foods, and abusing our trust. They use the gods to meet their own desires, twisting plain teachings into obscurities that can only be unlocked through their ignoble intercession." Jubal had some experience in this matter, having once played at honoring the gods of his land, admittedly to no advantage.

"What is more, our rulers are devils," Jubal continued, having some experience in this domain as well, "commanding by fear and by force, with the tax and with the sword. They are not leaders at all, but selfish brutes satisfying their vile lusts at the expense of the poor and helpless. They are slave masters, pure and simple." The musician's pent-up resentment had finally crested, and it slowly retreated as he rested his head on the table.

Mahijah had become nervous at his friend's warming ire, concerned that he might grow disrespectful or wake a sleeping child. But as he looked at Lamech, there was no apprehension to be seen. The farmer was as tranquil as ever, with a hint of indulgence, as if he had heard this very complaint more than once in the past.

Lamech agreed with the artist, using a soft voice to help calm his already dwindling fury. "It is true that men can be evil. It is in everyone's nature while we walk this earth to be selfish, carnal, egotistic, and devilish. But that is not our destiny. As you remember, we are free to choose our own path, and nothing or nobody—mortal or divine—can keep us from it. No—I misspeak—for we can equally choose afoul and remain bitter and self-seeking. That is our hazard as free agents. But a true and faithful Lawgiver reveals a spotless plan to overcome our nature and become new men and women in him. It centers on repentance, recognizing our faults and committing to overcome them through faith and education, but without the cultish elements you must have encountered in your old land. We in Zion have made our decision. We want to become pure in heart and action, purged of the wickedness that tries to overthrow us. We make a conscious decision—sometimes day to day—to be one-hearted with our neighbors and to live by the laws of our land. As we do so, we become our own masters, expanding our freedom and requiring fewer regulations or mortal rulers to govern us."

Mahijah could see that Jubal was still frustrated by the way he insisted on keeping his head low. The shepherd delivered to Lamech the questions he was sure the musician would have asked himself.

"You have said that Zion has no earthly king. This afternoon, we saw no soldiers in your streets. Do you mean to say that there are no magistrates to keep order, no mundane rules about exchanging goods, thieving, fighting, raping, or accidents? Are the inhabitants of Zion without flaw? It seems to me that having no laws but God's leaves every man to live by his own standard, but I did not detect a scent of anarchy along our route to dine at your house tonight."

"If all people were angels, we would need no law. We would make good decisions without fail, treating each other as ourselves," Lamech explained, tossing a date from the table into his mouth. "Such is our hope, our eventual end, but we have not arrived their just yet. We each fight evil tendencies daily, making amends when we lose a battle, forgiving ourselves for the shortcomings, and forging onward. Accidents are bound to happen, though we minimize them through our respect and care for each other. We do have some laws regarding such things, standards of measurement and guidelines for behavior, but they are more akin to generally understood best practices than to actual written regulations at this point. And there are not nearly as many now as there were when my mother was alive.

"We do have conflicts now and again, usually small matters that we resolve among ourselves, sometimes with the help of a neighbor unrelated to the incident to give us a clearer perspective. Once in a greater while, a significant matter is brought before one of our lower judges for a ruling, though I would have to check our annals to remember the last time that happened. I guess times are changing for the better! We find that the less we quarrel, the more time and energy we have for farming, improving our work techniques, music, writing, learning, and travel. We much prefer those pursuits. Do we not, my girls?"

Lamech took a break from his sermon to address his daughters, who were still by the far fire, now only embers. They had long abandoned their music and reading and had been lying prone on their bellies, chins cupped in their hands and feet swinging in the air, listening to their father. They had heard his words many times before, but enjoyed watching the reactions of their adopted uncles, a sight that itself was not novel to them. At their father's question, the younger girl nodded her head, but the older of the two groaned a bit, realizing that her father was really indicating in a roundabout way that it was time for bed.

"That is right, it is time for sleep. Come give me a hug, young ladies," their father admitted. At his request, the girls jumped up to embrace him, then said goodnight to the uncles at the low table.

Rising, the farmer said, "Friends, the candles are burning low and some are altogether out. Will you gather replacements? They are in the top drawer of the stand holding Enoch's book. I will see the children to bed."

The visitors rose to fulfill his request, Mahijah to fetch the candles and Jubal to replace the book. The musician spied Lamech's family record exactly where he had said it would be, on a lower shelf under the book of Enoch, and picked it up to take a look. It was constructed like the one he had just re-shelved, but thicker and with many different handwriting styles. He glanced at a number of the pages throughout the work, an assortment of letters, personal feelings, chronicles of family events, and frequent entries regarding city proceedings and related community news of days past. From what he could surmise, the city had been founded under humble circumstances over three hundred years ago, slowly growing from a small group of families living in low buildings to the glorious, populous center of industry that had already so impressed the two travelers.

Meanwhile, the shepherd walked throughout the room, replacing extinguished candles with fresh ones. He noted just how many candlesticks there were in the room, wondering to himself how affluent his host must be to afford so much light. He blew the rest of the candles around the room out, leaving only three at the table to radiate their convenient glows.

Mahijah sat back down on a cushion, his friend moving to join him, empty handed. With Lamech away, the travelers had the first opportunity since that morning to converse in private.

"What do you think?" the herdsman inquired, sitting at the low table and patting the cushion upon which his friend had been sitting earlier. "Zion seems too good to be true. No society can be as happy or as righteous as Lamech claims. Could it all be a ruse, a trick to take advantage of our situation? I wonder if the mule is safe. We have not heard a whinny from it the whole evening." He had abruptly become rather anxious, as if some malevolence had crept inside his mind unawares and threatened to sour his outlook.

"You cannot be serious, my friend," Jubal retorted, plopping down beside the cloak maker, sitting erect to give emphasis to his arguments.

"Would Lamech have brought us to his home, among his wife and babes, if he had intended to do us harm? No, he would have attacked us in the street after Zillah had left with the children near the gate, probably with help from conspirators. The notion is absurd! I am convinced he is genuine, at least in his belief. Never in Haner have I experienced such bona fide thoughtfulness from a stranger, and I am confident you will say the same of Sharon. Can you not tell that he has welcomed strangers in this manner before? You saw the counsel written in Enoch's book, and how it matched what we heard from *his* own mouth with *our* own ears. If you were to examine the second book even briefly as I just have, you would see decades—nearly centuries—of history to support what he is telling us. I perceive no deception in him, though I struggle a little to grasp all of his meaning. On the contrary, my heart is more at ease than at any time in my memory. Is not yours the same?"

"Yes, my heart is also at ease, I confess, regardless of the panic that overshadows me at times," Mahijah declared, calming himself. "But it is all just so fantastic, can you blame me for my doubts? Perhaps he will give us more clarity when he returns. I am not quite ready to retire."

As if on signal, Lamech walked through the threshold of the main room, rejoining his visitors. "Ah, thank you for your help," the farmer spoke in a loud whisper, looking about the room and then at the low table. "You are correct, we only need these few candles to close our discussion, unless it has ended already. We have covered a lot of concepts on full stomachs. Do you have anything further to ask of me?"

"You indulge us too much, I think, but as I am still eager, please allow one thing more," Jubal requested, reclining again on the cushions and suggesting to the farmer that he retake his place. "Tell us, with no king, how does Zion order itself in its legal affairs?"

"This question has been mostly answered in our exchange already, though I am happy to elucidate. The best explanation is that we govern ourselves, under divine tutelage. Preachers teach us correct principles, and we endeavor to follow them. They persuade and plead with us to do what is right, and then leave us alone to act as seems us good. Enoch is currently our chief judge, being elected by the voice of the people, though we rarely see him in that capacity. Only when he defends us against an aggressor, or resolves some pressing matter the lower judges cannot handle, does he put on that mantle. Otherwise, when he is not serving as a scribe or tending his garden at home, he is off to foreign lands preaching God's word. He is traveling now on that errand, apparently in nations to our north based on your accounting, and not expected to return for another few weeks, I think. I will have to ask him about his squash when he returns. He grows the most delicate orange squash I have ever tasted! It puts my efforts to shame, I must admit. The way he does it is pure genius. He breeds a yellow plant with a …"

"You stated that your leader is elected? What does that mean?" Jubal interrupted, more interested in Enoch's position as judge than in his gardening techniques, though the shepherd had been curious to hear the gardening practice.

"Oh, yes, of course. Apologies. I do love talking shop, but that will save for another day. Elected, right. We have a chief judge in Zion who makes rulings for the entire land, and then lower judges as needed for smaller divisions within the city. Every man and woman who has reached the age of thirty years is considered mature enough to participate in deciding who will be our leaders, or to become a judge herself. We vote whenever a leader dies, or steps down from her office, or when at least a fifth of the population feels the need for a change. A potential judge does not put herself forward for the position, but must be nominated by twenty percent of the residents she would represent. Only nominees receiving two out of every three votes becomes a magistrate, and a popular vote of at least four in five can overrule the specific decision of any official, but I do not think we have ever relied on that recourse. A larger group of twelve members forms a council to preside over criminal accusations against any one of the judges.

"Once confirmed by the voice of the people, magistrates each receive a token of money for the time they sit in judgement, then return to their houses and regular professions when matters have been resolved.

We do not see much of our judges in their official capacity these days, as I already mentioned. That is really about all there is to our structure. Sometimes, groups will ask an official to serve with other men and women on temporary committees for events, or to make recommendations about constructing new buildings, but even that is rare. Whenever some project requiring a group effort arises, the involved inhabitants just figure it out together. They might get counsel from a judge, infrequently paying her to make a pronouncement for them, but even then the magistrates refer to the word of God and ask the parties if they cannot come to a solution on their own."

Lamech offered final cups of water to his friends, filled his own for the last time, and capped the pitcher with a clay lid that had some shiny blue cloth attached to it. He was growing tired.

"So, Enoch must be rich! How can he claim to be the poorest man in Zion if he receives tribute as your highest magistrate?" Jubal stifled his cry, suddenly sensitive to the quiet around him. He could not be blamed for his outburst as he was relying on knowledge from his past life, where power and wealth intermingled, the one being both a prerequisite and result of the other.

"Ah, he loves to call himself that, *the poorest man in Zion*. Nobody enjoys a clever pun more than he, from what I have heard," Lamech laughed lightly, a distant look in his eye that quickly faded. "Such is his privilege, but I will let him explain that for himself when he returns. Rest assured, you will not find more silver or gold in his modest house than you will in my own."

"What of crime?" Mahijah asked with a weary voice. His attention was waning, and his eyes growing heavy, but he had one last question to submit for consideration. "If the people of Zion are not yet angels, what happens when they succumb to their lesser natures?"

"When we make mistakes or cause accidents, we must take responsibility for our actions. We make restitution between the guilty and the aggrieved so that all are appeased. When the parties are not satisfied, or when a person refuses to be accountable, the lower judges are called upon to pass sentence. A judge compels witnesses for both parties to appear and declare in honesty their perception of the conflict. She employs knowledge and wisdom to render verdicts, relying on her own reflections and inquiries as needed, always being slow and cautious in her deliberations. We do not tolerate false accusations, lying, or vicious gossip, and prosecute them the same as other crimes. If needed, the accused is bound until a judgement can be declared, but that is always temporary, for we have no prisons in our city. If innocent, the accused immediately goes free and the accuser is encouraged to join her in the hand of friendship. Throughout the process, support and education for all involved parties are emphasized to avoid future issues.

"If guilty, the offender is disciplined. This almost always takes the form of a payment to compensate the victim, such as for destruction or theft of property, with added financial penalties to discourage repeated misconduct. If the convicted declines to make the required payment, then equivalent labor is allowed until the debt is repaid, sometimes through a third party willing to receive assistance from the penitent. If labor is refused, or when more violent crimes are committed, stripes are exacted on the back of the guilty as an extra chastisement, but never more than forty. The judge has great discretion in allocating punishment, balancing mercy with justice.

"In the most severe of cases, a person's life may be required, but that has never been the situation in Zion since our founding. The sternest sentence I can remember ever occurring was banishment from the land, and then only for those found guilty but remaining unrepentant. Despite the loving help of their family and friends, they refused to change their ways after being reproved for multiple affronts. They would not depart of their own accord, so they were asked to leave.

"But on occasion, those guilty of past offenses return to us and are welcomed with open arms. As soon as they have atoned for their past crimes, they are integrated back into our community. Those are joyous days indeed! In any case, once repentance is considered complete, forgiveness is freely extended and our fellow is restored to our society, unblemished.

But in all this remember: we govern ourselves and resolve nearly all of our conflicts among neighbors. We cannot have our esteemed judges wasting their time resolving petty disputes when their talents might be applied to more noble and pleasing vocations."

Lamech finished his cup, then gave his guests an admiring look. The evening was well-spent, and they were visibly drained from their discussion. He saw in them the hope that he had witnessed in strangers of former days who had passed through the gates of his city, in his step-father on the eve of his marriage, in some cases in the faces of his own children. He felt love for them and wanted nothing less than for his new friends to feel that love. Maybe one day they would, but for now it was rest that they needed. He would see to it.

"Please, Jubal and Mahijah, I am exhausted. Should we not retire?" Lamech stood stiffly, not waiting for an answer and pointing to one of the openings off of the main room. "Your bedroom is just through that door and on the left hand. You will find all you require. I wish you a long and sound sleep. Tomorrow, the family is working in the fields again and we must leave early, but our house is yours. You will find meat and water to spare, with plenty of soft hay in the barn. Relax as many days as you wish, exercise your mule, explore the city, and meet new friends. We can speak again over dinner tomorrow night."

"You have given us so much to consider that we can barely grasp it," Jubal expressed his gratitude, including the shepherd in his thanks. The artist had quickly become comfortable speaking for the older man, who returned nothing but approval. "We are ever in your debt, and would risk a greater liability if you will allow it. We will not impose on you again tomorrow, as your schedule is already full, but since you spoke of the community within Zion, can you recommend someone for us to visit? There is still much to learn of your nation. Enoch is the only other soul we know in all of your city, and if he be away, might you introduce us to another person who would be willing to entertain visitors in his place?"

"Hmmm ..." Lamech reflected on the request for a moment. "That sounds like a good idea. I suspect our local judge would be available, but let me offer you another option. There is a stonemason, Joshua, who lives not far from here and to whom I owe a delivery. I must provide direction in the fields, as you know, but I can spare my daughter, Naamah, for a portion of the morning to escort you to him. She will be your guide and my courier. I will speak to her before leaving in the morning."

"Thank you, Lamech, but I think we prefer to speak to someone more about Zion and less about masonry. As you know, we seek information to heal our souls, not to work our hands." Jubal prayed that he did not seem ungrateful.

"I would suggest the work of our hands are needed as much as the intent of our hearts. But no worries, my dear Jubal. I am sure that you and Mahijah will have much to discuss with Joshua. He is a stonemason by trade, but his calling is to serve Zion in financial matters. He knows more about hard work—its merits and challenges—than the average resident within our walls. He can teach you all about the inner workings of our economy. Your souls will be filled by the time you join us for dinner tomorrow evening, unless you decide to abide with Joshua instead."

"Then we will make that our plan. It is a good one," concluded Mahijah, picking up the final thread in their conversation. "Tomorrow, we dissect the economies of Zion. I will feed and water the mule in the morning before Naamah leads us to Joshua. With his permission, we will sit at his feet as the earnest pupils you know us to be. We will then return to your house for dinner, or send word of our absence.

"It is a minor thing, but as we follow our design, being true to our plans for tomorrow, it will give us good practice at keeping to our word. We may not be ready to follow the ways of Zion in total just yet, but we can at least do what we know in our hearts to be virtuous. Consider it our tiny contribution to establishing righteousness."

PROMISING GOALS
DRIVE ACTION

5

THE LABORER IS WORTHY OF HIS HIRE

JUBAL WAS RESTED. HE HAD never slept so soundly, yet another pearl in a string of unique events he was experiencing since he conspired to pursue lasting happiness. By the time he awakened and pulled himself from bed, the sun was well above the horizon. His friend had already vacated the second, straw-filled cushion in their host's amply-large guest bedroom. It had been left empty—neatly made—though how long ago the musician could not be positive. Mahijah, the shepherd, must have already risen and ventured to the barn to care for his mule, perhaps to check on the robes and scraps of cloth it had carried on their journey, and to review their scant provisions leftover from more than six days of arduous desert travel.

Unfortunately, Jubal held no such concerns, possessing nothing of value in the world but his flute of nine pipes, which still lay next to his plush, appropriated pillow. He was dressed in his only clothing, worn and ripped from over use, no sandals to call his own. He owned no dwelling place, possessed no living family, and had no real business being in this recently-discovered, alien land.

Pieces of yesterday started to drift through his mind, and he exhaled deeply. He had not realized just how exhausted he was after the intense conversation of last night and now felt a little embarrassed for staying abed this late into the morning. His awkwardness gave way to agitation as he remembered the commitment he and Mahijah had made to

Lamech, their host and new brother in the City of Zion.

And there it was!

Jubal's chest swelled with gratitude as he recognized that he was not as poor as he thought. The privations of his past mattered little, for he did have his old friend to offer aid, when he needed it, and his new friends to offer motivation and meaning for his life, a desire to continue. He was in reasonably good health with a full belly and a head full of wonderful possibilities. He also held the honor of his faithful word, something that for many years he had not cared about keeping.

His pledge was to visit a stonemason within the city to learn the economies of this spectacular society he and Mahijah had come to explore. He was determined to be true to his promise of last night, knowing that it was an important thing—a good thing—to be as honest as possible. As the herdsman would undoubtedly remind him, he was free to be true or not, but they both had learned that the path to happiness was paved with good decisions, and he desperately wanted to be happy.

The musician carefully made his borrowed bed, following the example of his aged friend, and walked sunnily into the main room of Lamech's dwelling. There was Naamah, one of the many daughters of the farmer, busy with some chores. She was clothed in a brown dress that fell to her calves, with a bright green sash around her waist. He saw Mahijah, his slender friend and traveling companion, at the low table in the center of the chamber, closely reading from the book of Enoch. Lamech's family history book was also opened, resting off to one side of the herdsman.

The girl noticed his arrival and smiled at his entrance, running over to give him a great hug about the waist and then hold his hand. Her movement jostled the older uncle from his study.

"There he is!" exclaimed the cloak maker. "If not for your tremendous snoring, I would have thought you had died in your sleep! I could hear you from the end of the passage that leads to our guest room. Are you well? It looks like you are ready for a brand new day."

"If I had perished in my sleep, it would have been a pleasant passing. I do not know if I ever shared this with you, but, for many months after the war, my fondest wish had been to die peacefully in the night while lying prone in the street."

Jubal felt an anxious tug at his arm and gathered that his language may have been inappropriate for Naamah to hear. She suddenly had a sad look on her face and was silently shaking her head back and forth.

"Oh my dear child!" he exhaled in a rush as he bent down to reassure her, easily hefting her slight but vigorous frame into his arms. "Naamah, do not worry about your uncle. That was a sad time, back when I was lonely and angry. I was scared, really—and actually quite selfish now that I think of it."

Turning to face the shepherd at the low table, he spoke to them both. "Yes, I am well. Those days are all behind me now, for I have already learned enough to make dramatic changes in my life—changes for the better. For one, I am elated to know that I have a pretty niece who cares about my welfare, even though I met her just yesterday. Will you fetch me some cool water to clear my raspy throat?"

The musician lowered the girl, merry once more, and she ran to the kitchen, leaving Jubal to reflect on what had led him to this day. Raised in a loving family, Jubal was content as a child, investing most of his days training himself to play the flute. His mastery of music represented the single largest effort of his young life and indirectly helped him survive the surprise onslaught of the aggressive king of Heni just two years ago. His wife and the family of his youth were not as fortunate, carried off captive or buried under the rubble of Haner's broken outer walls, a portion of which served as his father's residence. Combined with the struggles of wealth, followed by the tussles of poverty, he gave up on just about everything. He was begging in the dust and filth of his city streets when he bumped into Mahijah and his fortune began to change. Their natural friendship slowly renewed Jubal's courage, prompting him to return, if hesitantly, to the melodies of his instrument.

For his part, the shepherd was still glad for the attachment, for he had struggled with loneliness and discouragement his whole life. Raised in the land of Sharon, his mother perished giving birth to him, and he bore the blame for his family's loss until they all either died of famine or abandoned him to the cold. When the wife and children of his later years starved, too weak to survive the latest shortage, he finally moved to Haner and took up residence in a vacant house outside the walls, left empty when its owners had been slaughtered by the army of Heni. His skill at nurturing sheep and sewing cloaks from their wool was his only company until he befriended Jubal. The relationship was a blessing to both. If Jubal was slow to acknowledge it, Mahijah was less so, for the wiser man recognized without question the void in his life and wished to replace it with some degree of satisfaction. He needed a genuine human connection. He wanted to be happy.

Their growing companionship was augmented eight days ago when Mahijah persuaded the artist to hike to the western gate of Haner and listen to the words of Enoch, the prophet of Zion. He was a wandering preacher to some and a wicked vagrant and slanderer to others, but as far as the two friends were concerned, the seer was their savior. He taught them the first principles of true happiness, then sent them on their way to the one place they were guaranteed to find it.

They had arrived just yesterday morning in the fields north of the city gate and encountered Naamah and her family for the first time. Now, they were in the city itself, guests of a trusting and compassionate farmer, his lovely wife, and their many polite children.

"Now, though … now," Jubal spoke in a soft voice, pausing thoughtfully, then becoming more forceful as he stood in the main room of the dwelling. "Now everything is different. I want to live, but more than that, I want to live *fully*. The words of Enoch and Lamech have given me resolve, Mahijah. I can tell you feel the same. We must see Joshua as we have promised. He will teach us even more, and if possible, strengthen our resolve to discover new joy."

Mahijah looked back down at the table and gently folded the copy of Enoch's book he was reading, respectfully placing it to one side. He carefully slid the family journal in front of him to take the place of the first volume.

"You are correct as always, young uncle. I have spent the morning between these two books, and the feelings of my heart are more firmly confirmed as a result. The principles in Enoch's book ring true to me," he said while pointing to the closed book on the low table. Then, tapping the pages of the family archives, he explained, "and this book supplies ample evidence of those very principles in action. It is really quite incredible to learn of how the city and its inhabitants have evolved. I would be thrilled to compare accounts from other families and the public record with this history, but that will have to wait for another time. We should depart as soon as we can to meet the stonemason."

The young girl returned to the chamber with a pitcher and a cup for the musician, placed them on the table, then walked over and reached up to squeeze him a second time. "All is readied for us to leave on our walk. Uncle Mahijah and I have already had breakfast. Would you also like something to eat before we go?"

"No child, I am still full from the feast of last night. How can you eat like that every evening? All of your brothers and sisters must have hollow legs! Just some water to wash down the dust and I am ready to set out. Let us go meet our next friend."

He poured one drink, then a second, before the girl took the pitcher and the cup from him, returning them to their proper locations and reappearing almost instantly. The cloak maker closed the history he had been reading, then took both books in hand, rose from the table, and walked over to the wooden stand where they were stored, laying them down with an air of affection. With everything back in place, the trio left the main room, navigated some passages through the dwelling, and exited the familiar front door.

Naamah grabbed each adopted uncle with one of her hands, then started to skip through the streets, the men easily keeping stride with her short steps. While the lass was at perfect ease with the uncles, the arrangement was surreal for them. Not only were they in the welcome company of a young girl they barely knew—her father having conveyed to them his total trust for her safety—but they were back in the peculiar and generous streets of Zion.

They found the avenues to be as remarkable in the new morning light as they had been in the dying twilight, only now they were even busier with activity. The same kind of vibrant people the uncles had seen yesterday were once more walking in all directions, stopping to talk with their fellow residents, smiling and laughing. There were some older men over in a corner, having what appeared to be a serious exchange about pig herding techniques. An assembly of comely ladies in high-quality outfits of various vibrant, though unassuming, colors and patterns—regular dress, it seemed, for all the occupants of the city—were in the midst of an animated dialogue of their own. Upon spotting other women walking alone in the lane, they would urge their sisters to join their group, including them in the discussion as if they had been involved from the beginning.

Some boys were playing in the street, rolling wheeled toys down gentle slopes. Some girls were off to one side, amusing themselves by throwing small pebbles at a circled target on a wall that was otherwise decorated with ornate carvings. Sunburned men carrying baskets full of fish were strolling through the way, casually announcing their catches for sale with bass and tenor voices, their helpful sons and daughters collecting coins from passing customers. The scenes were so natural that the uncles supposed them to be commonplace.

The visitors soon grasped that they were unwitting contributors to the very scenery they had been observing. Naamah was apparently known by just about everyone the three of them passed in the street. All along their way, men and women—children, too—would see Naamah and say *hello*. Those with some extra time in their day, or with a more robust curiosity, would stop the girl and her escorts to ask about her mother and father, brothers and sisters. She would present her new uncles and give them a chance to introduce themselves more fully. They would end up explaining how they came to visit the city and how they were going to see Joshua, details that their new acquaintances were glad to receive.

Progress to their appointment was slow because of this constant attention, but Naamah was accustomed to it, acting as if it were a normal occurrence. Jubal and Mahijah were astounded by the comradery and intimacy afforded such a young girl by those they would have supposed to be interested in more serious affairs.

Turning a corner, the trio happened upon a spacious, teeming marketplace where residents gathered to trade merchandise, gather news, and enjoy company. It was certainly busy, and from their initial assessment, as large a crowd as ever the travelers had witnessed. But once they started walking through it to visit the booths and tents on display, it did not seem very crowded at all. Due to the sheer volume of shoppers, the noise in the bazaar was definitely louder than that in the streets, but not unpleasantly so. The arrangement of the area gave plenty of space for buyers and sellers alike, and the noise dissipated into the open sky above as if by design. The whole affair radiated a deliberate structure—a regulated order, with stalls aligning into rows and columns, and with walkways in between—proving that it was practiced to some degree.

Friendly merchants were selling all kinds of goods, colorful signs and cheerful voices announcing the particulars. The visitors could not make much sense of the transactions, for it seemed the proprietors valued their goods well below their true worth. But there was no shouting nor haranguing, and what little haggling they witnessed was entirely good-natured. Food, wines, tools, bedding, shoes and clothing, furniture, animals, artwork, household items, farming implements, construction gear—the list of things for trade went on and on. The sheer quantity and variety of offered items was hard to believe, and the quality appeared to be superior to any they had observed in Haner. The uncles supposed that the wealth of Zion must be astonishing.

Mahijah looked down at their guide and asked, "Is this a designated market day, since so many customers are roaming the square? Maybe there is a celebration for some special occurrence in the city?"

Naamah furrowed her brow in thought. "What is this, the second day of the week? No … I cannot think of anything special going on. Oh wait, it is my friend's birthday today! Her house is down the street from ours, not far away at all. I will bring her a gift tonight after dinner, when she gets back from helping with her father's goats in the meadows. Other than that, just a regular day as far as I know."

The shepherd laughed out loud, and the artist could not help but joining him in the joke. Naamah was confused to how her friend's birthday was funny, but she laughed as well.

Mahijah turned to the musician and said, "I doubt that all of this excitement could be for a goat herder's little daughter. It must be just as Naamah said: another regular day in Zion."

"Oh, the performers!" Naamah squealed, dragging her uncles with her towards a dissimilar type of bustling activity straight ahead.

The friends were happy to follow their cute attendant down the main aisle of the bazaar, especially when they saw where she was leading them. The trading center in this area was peppered with street artists and entertainers of every kind, offering their talents for the market-goers to see and hear. Singers, dancers, a sculpturer in the middle of her most recent work, a magician dazzling a small crowd with his sleight of hand, all graced stages of their own making. There was no dearth of entertainment to view.

Some of the performers would end their displays by passing around a hat, or a bag of some kind, soliciting a small reward from those who had appreciated their show. Not everyone donated, but those who did were liberal with their gifts. Even the young Naamah pulled a few silver coins from the unpretentious sack secured at her waist—compensation for her favorite artists. Regardless of the exchanges taking place, there was never a scowl or angry word among the parties, everyone appearing to be comfortable with the give and take being presented.

Other performers handed out leaflets announcing upcoming events or opportunities to enjoy their crafts, expecting nothing in return. The whole spectacle was a delight for the girl to watch and astounding for her uncles to consider that it could even exist.

By contrast, the uncles were unable to locate any bad actors of the sort they were accustomed to seeing in the city and byways of their homeland. As in the streets leading to the square, there were no signs of strife, malice, or theft—no drunkards in the corners, nor gambling in the shadows, nor pickpockets among the throng. Children there were a plenty, but only a rare few gathered under foot in a bothersome way, and they were promptly forgiven before parents could apologize to their fellow market-goers. They did see a man with a sword about his waist and a helmet in his hand, stretching his neck here and there to view his surroundings, but it was immediately clear that he was looking for something to purchase, not monitoring the crowd for villains. The apparent safety of the city and its bustling market was conceivably why a young girl felt no fear in walking its streets with a bag of silver.

As fascinating as the experience was, Jubal remembered the reason for their travel that morning and was about to suggest the trio continue to their destination—until he spied the flute player.

Jubal was the first to notice the instrumentalist to the left of the main aisle, a modest podium under her feet allowing her audience a better view of her performance. She was playing a light and contemplative tune as he approached, dragging his companions behind him, drawn powerlessly to the lilt of the notes trickling from her large flute. He stood in front of her small perch, staring in awe with his companions beside him.

She held in her hand an impressive pan flute, similar in construction to Jubal's, though it was of much finer construction. It measured a full thirteen pipes, the most lengthy nearly reaching her waist. It was carefully crafted from soft wood and held together by a golden metal that shined like copper, but was more yellow in color. From it flowed a celebration of music that reminded him of the annual harvest festival he had attended with his parents. It was light and upbeat, and ended too soon for his liking.

He was anxious to speak with the artist, to ask questions and compare her training and experiences with his own, but wrestled his impatience into submission. He waited until her tune rose to the anticipated finale and her audience broke out into a loud applause. He joined in their clapping, but abruptly lost confidence in what to say. As Jubal tried to gather his thoughts, appreciative listeners dropped pieces of money into a woven basket near the young lady's feet in grateful response to her show.

"Do you have a question about my music?" the young lady asked, reviving Jubal from his awkward reverie. She had noticed him in front of her, staring in silence, unsure of what he might want.

"Oh, yes! Wait—I mean *no*," Jubal stammered, a little embarrassed by the way he had become enthralled with her music. "What I intended to say was that your song was so beautiful. It reminded me of one of my own pieces from home. Did you compose it yourself? Who made your flute? Its range is so low and high, it must afford a tremendous number of possibilities in performing. Do you know where I can find one for myself? Will you play another song?"

Mahijah placed a calming hand on his friend's shoulder, hoping to relieve the musician of some of his nervousness. The grayed man smiled at the female flutist as if to reassure her that Jubal's excitement was innocent. The young lady smiled back at the shepherd, unruffled by the attention given her, then turned to answer Jubal.

"Why thank you for your compliments. I am still apprenticing with my master, but I love playing. She says I will soon be ready—by the end of the month—for a full concert, though I *must* keep practicing. This belongs to her, but my father will soon finish the one he is making for me. Only the final touches remain, from what he tells me. Do you play?"

Jubal quickly shook the remaining clumsiness from his voice to respond. "*Do I play?* Uh, not a simple question for me to answer. I *used* to play, for small crowds and large, even before the king of my country, but not as well as you have this morning. I was considered the best in my whole city, though you have shown me in a few minutes how far I might still advance in our craft. I am impressed that you have mastered so much at such a young age. May I try your flute?"

Jubal regretted his request as soon as he had made it, considering it an impulsive entreaty that would make the young lady uncomfortable. But she was as poised and self-assured as her music was melodic. He was surprised at her forthright consent, receiving the instrument from her light grip without evasion.

He took it with two hands and examined it carefully, touching every pipe with his fingers, then placed his lips to them. With a deep breath, he closed his eyes and started to play one of his own, favorite tunes. It was a song simple in its construction, but he was stunned at how rich and full it sounded on this impressive flute. As he finished, the young lady's crowd applauded again, but for *him* this time. A tinkle of coins could be heard in the young lady's basket once more.

"Without mistake, you are no novice. Your talent is obvious. Will you join my recital at the end of the month? Our neighbors would be thrilled to have us both play," declared the young lady as she stooped down to reach into her basket, then stood back erect, waiting for his answer.

Jubal was not sure how to react. The flutist did not even know him and now she was offering to share her stage with him? Who in their right mind does that sort of thing? Setting her unexpected generosity aside, to perform again would be a great joy, of course, but was his heart ready for that? Could he ever be ready for that?

"Well, here are the details, whatever you decide," said the young lady, noticing Jubal's delay in responding. She handed him an announcement with the specifics of her upcoming recital.

"And here are your earnings. I hope to see you once more—and soon." Without waiting for a refusal—or a *thank you*, for that matter—she placed four silver coins in his hand, then immediately started playing again. This time, the song was a livelier tune evidently known to her supporters, for they began clapping their hands in time with it.

The musician was astonished again, for he had not held silver in his hands for years. He opened the tiny purse he kept out of habit at his waist and carefully dropped his compensation into it. Back in the streets of Haner, earning this much money would have taken him a full month of playing to the crowds. But it only took one song to earn as much in Zion. This young lady—these people—were undoubtedly the richest of all the societies in the region, and the most charitable as well. What a delight it was for Jubal, in his tiny way, to participate in the adventure!

His exploit reminded him of their original aim of learning about

Zion's pecuniary principles. "Naamah, let us go. We have lingered too long when there are obligations to be met. Take us to the stonemason. We must keep our promise."

Jubal took the girl softly by the hand and led her through the crowds once more, his tall friend following behind them. As pleasing as their distraction had been in the bazaar, he was once more focused on their goal, and he would persist in that vein until all three had arrived at their destination as they had planned.

From a distance, the building they sought looked similar to the one owned by Lamech the farmer, but as they grew closer the uncles could tell that it was significantly different. Yes, it was well-built and strong, tidy and attractive like Lamech's residence, but the construction was unique and the footprint was much smaller, with no apparent shed for livestock. There were three enormous, cubed structures off to the side, but they did not appear to be related to the house. A considerable courtyard spilled out in front of the structures, with basic benches and a few small trees along its walled edges. The front door was squared instead of arched, made of a dark, plain wood instead of the light, tan color of the farmer's dwelling.

The young girl ran up to the door and knocked boldly. When an older man answered, she yelled *Joshua*, and gave him a hefty squeeze about his waist, as was her habit.

Joshua the stonemason was clean-shaven, red-haired like Jubal, and taller than most men. Skinny like Mahijah, barefooted and with an uncovered head, he looked older than Lamech, but not by much. His hands were calloused and scarred from years of working stone. His clothing was plain and simple, though the cloak maker discerned it was of a long-lasting quality that would guarantee decades of use.

He spoke slowly and reflectively, not as impulsively as Lamech. The stonemason and the farmer were as unlike each other as night is from day in many respects, though similar in those that mattered the most. As the two uncles would soon discover, their hosts shared the same motivations, the same attitudes towards service and love. And they both welcomed the chance to talk about Zion.

"How is my sparkling friend, Naamah, this morning?" Joshua asked, lowering his chin to see the girl who had just released him from her friendly embrace. He bent down to be even with her face as she stood in the doorway. "And who are your friends you bring to meet with me this fine day?"

Naamah giggled like little girls sometimes do. "We saw performers in the market! That was fun, but now I need to go help father with our farm. These are my new uncles, Jubal and Mahijah, visiting from outside the city. They spoke with father all night, and now they have come to speak with you. I must go help before mother misses me too much. We finish the date harvesting today. Oh … and father asked me to give you this."

She reached for the sash around her waist that complemented her work dress and handed to the man a small coin purse, the same from which she had drawn coins while in the marketplace. She then gave her uncles a last hug, said goodbye to all, and ran off to join her family in the fields.

As the two travelers walked towards the door, Jubal felt obliged to furnish a more detailed explanation. "We are not in truth her uncles, but merely travelers from Haner come to learn about this people. We spoke with Enoch the missionary eight days ago and he taught us about your God and his city, suggesting we see it for ourselves. Has it been only eight days? It feels like a lifetime! We became acquainted with Lamech and his family yesterday, and spent the night in his care. He recommended we speak to you about how business is run in the land, you being an expert of some sort."

"Well, any friend of Naamah is welcome here. Please, come in and be at ease," Joshua responded, holding the door open and motioning for his guests to join him in the house. They walked directly into the main room of the structure, and started to look around, but their good-natured host kept their attention.

"I presume that I am an expert of one sort or another. Are not we all? Some might say my proficiency is in financial matters, but do not *dare* to take their word for it. You will have to judge that for yourself. Right now, I am wrapping up some business with my dear sister in the other chamber and must leave you, but the fire here is warm, and you will find wine on the table over there. I will not be long."

The uncles watched Joshua leave the chamber, placing the sack of coins in the center of the low table as he did so. They were instantly relaxed as they walked to the center of the room, but not due exclusively to the courtesy of their host. The familiarity of their surroundings also contributed to their comfort, for the guests were unmistakably reminded of Lamech's dwelling, though struggled to understand exactly why. As they had noted from outside, the two houses were clearly not identical. Joshua's house was much smaller; it displayed no courtyard, fewer chambers, and a tiny kitchen area, though with taller ceilings. It was quieter, with more refined decorations if fewer of them. No animals were kept, and there was no barn to be seen.

Mahijah did see against one wall a wooden stand, similar to that in Lamech's house that supported the book of Enoch, and pointed it out to his friend. He walked to the rack and sure enough, there was a book of similar construction atop it, and on a lower shelf a second volume that must be a comparable family archive. Still, the books could not account for the sense of familiarity.

Then Mahijah understood. It was the *feeling* of the house that was familiar: peaceful and orderly, open and candid. He turned to the musician and said, "I wonder if all homes are like this in the city. You feel it too, do you not?"

Jubal nodded as he spoke. "Yes, I do. An odd sensation, mild and inviting. I cannot wait to hear what Joshua will teach us."

He sat on the colorful floor cushions next to the low table, poured cups of wine for himself and the cloak maker, then relaxed in the stillness waiting for the return of the expert. The shepherd joined him, sampling assorted nuts from a small bowl on the same table.

Before long, Joshua re-entered the room with his *sister*, an elderly and distinguished lady with a broad grin who acted more like a grandmother than a sibling. She paused to introduce herself and chat for a few minutes before the stonemason escorted her out the front door. He closed it behind him and came to sit with his visitors at the low table, pouring a cup of wine for himself.

"Now, tell me in more detail what brings you to our fine city. Is my friend Enoch well? You say you saw him last week and he spoke with you? What news can you share?"

Joshua was in no hurry, so the visitors obliged, taking turns relating their desire for lasting happiness, their experience with the evangelist, the beginning of their trip, and all they had discussed with Lamech the day and night before.

"You have learned much already, it seems, of our ways in Zion. I am delighted to add to your education. But first, please realize: happiness can be found in any land, in any condition, as long as you are practicing the principles that lead to it. We who live in this city have chosen to gather together so that our joy might be even greater, and so that we might achieve more as a team. Nonetheless, some of us elect to live in other lands for the short periods, among friends and family and strangers, to influence them for the better. Zion is a disposition of the heart as much as a physical location. Blessed are they who experience both."

"Please, Joshua," the shepherd implored, "tell us more of your fiscal customs. We have seen the precious works on your outer walls and the splendor of your gate, unmatched in our joint experience. We have witnessed the wonders of the bazaar on our way to your house. We expect to see nothing equal to it in Sharon, or Haner, or in any lands in the region. Your people must be wealthy beyond measure."

Mahijah was sincere in his compliment, and Joshua in his thanks for it.

"Yes, my friend, your words are exact," the stonemason confirmed. "We are the wealthiest city in the widespread world, but our silver and gold are only a small piece of that prosperity, as you must assuredly have noticed. I do however, need to correct you in one regard, for you very well might see an equal to the marketplace you so recently enjoyed. There is another, nearly identical to it, on the southern side of the city."

Joshua finished his wine and turned his cup upside down, wiping the corners of his mouth. He looked at one visitor, then the other, and back to the first without feeling the need to say anything further.

The travelers sat in silence, jaws agape. If the one bazaar alone was greater than any they had ever seen, and there was a second such square within the boundaries of the land, then the pilgrims *truly* underestimated the city's fortune. To be the poorest man in Zion, as Enoch had claimed the day they sought him out, may not be such a drawback. Such a person would *still* possess riches to rival any king. The expression on their faces clearly signaled that they were not quite prepared to say anything more.

"I see you are surprised," Joshua continued, "but there is no great mystery to our affluence. As you have already learned, individual freedom is the basis of it. Our unified vision and thoughtful commitment to choosing the right—dedication to heavenly goals—are also key elements, for how could we flourish when lacking the motivation and strategies to do so? But none of that is helpful unless we act. The root cause of our prosperity, the reason we thrive while other societies barely survive, is as practical as it is sustainable. It is as unassuming as it is effective. It is plainly this: hard work."

"Can it be that simple?" Jubal asked, full of skepticism. He knew that the occupants of Haner worked, some of them diligently so, but they were cursed with poverty. Mahijah was equally unconvinced, for he had toiled all of his life and always been deprived of great wealth.

"I believe it is," Joshua continued. "A free person with motivation and some kind of a plan will still achieve nothing without hard work. But *with* hard work, it is possible for a person to attain some level of success *even* if her freedom is limited, she lacks vision, and she fails to grasp the need for strategic planning.

"Industry is the basis of our economy. It was the first commandment given to our father, Adam, when he was physically formed: to work the land and to take good care of what he received. That divine direction stands to this day. Wealth is created as men and women labor in the garden, raising cattle, building roads or houses or public auditoriums, creating art, and devising new methods or practices. It is produced as we become experts in mechanics or in medicine or in any of countless other fields of endeavor, and as we teach others the knowledge, skills, and fruitful habits we have acquired.

"Through the sweat of our brows, we add value to our community in innumerable ways. Everyone contributes in one manner or another—some with our hands, others with our minds, still others with our voices, but all with our hearts. We are free to choose the profession we prefer, maybe because it gives us gratification in and of itself, or because we are skilled at it and find joy in developing that skill. But we must also accept the risks inherent in pursuing it. We might start in one area of work, then change to another that suits us better. All earnest efforts have worth, and we are each so varied in our likes and wants that there is no end to the collection of occupations from which we benefit.

"Indolence, on the other hand, has no place among us. I speak not of well-deserved respites, for we all must rest and recover from our labors. Leisure activities, even sedate ones, are valuable. Think back to your journeys in our streets and in the bazaar. Did you see any loafing, laziness, or idle gaming? Was time and energy being wasted? I certainly hope not! All who are able to work pitch in based on their choices and market demands, and we are better for it.

"The contentment and joy you saw at the bazaar, and with Lamech on his farm, are natural results of our labors. By and large, we want to contribute to our mutual benefit. It is satisfying in itself to create something through our efforts, but how much more fulfilling is work when we see our family and friends taking pleasure in it as well! When we first prosper individually, we are then able to prosper collectively."

Jubal found his voice. "But if one person prospers, does that not mean another must suffer? Even in such a large city, there cannot be demand for all the fruits and grains your many farmers grow. Do not envy and discord rise in the hearts of once-dear neighbors when they learn they are actually competitors for favor in the marketplace?"

"Your questions are perceptive, uncle," Joshua observed. He was enjoying their conversation, but needed something more to drink with all of his talking. He disappeared from the chamber briefly, reappearing with a second pitcher—this one of water—and poured himself a cup, swallowing it in one motion. He was now ready to answer.

"Yes, it is true, we are all competing against each other for business, but it is a friendly opposition, one that makes everyone stronger, smarter, and happier. It might be like some of the athletic contests we enjoy in our society. Consider that in a footrace, someone will arrive at the finish line first, another second, and another third until the last. At the end of the race, they all rejoice in the results and receive honor and recognition commensurate with their rankings, sometimes corresponding to their efforts, too. True, the first place competitor might receive the highest honor, but second place receives her earned degree of praise as well. Even the last place runner receives acclaim for finishing the race and contributing to the sport. It is not an all or nothing affair.

"They then return to their training to get ready for the next footrace. The one arriving last pushes herself for improvement, while the one arriving first drives herself to preserve the honor she has earned. The rivalry is a blessing, for it spurs everyone involved to advance her craft. The runners will often practice together, directly encouraging each other, respectfully sharing tips and techniques to shave seconds from their times. We exhibit and retain our greatest talent through the help of our loving competitors. You should see how our racers celebrate in the city after a contest, sharing a meal, congratulating each other, openly recounting their feats and failings with humor and hugs, making plans for the next race. They are legitimate allies.

"So is our daily business. We contend with each other to deliver the best products, the most efficient processes, the most compelling advertising, and the lowest prices. We measure success by satisfying current and new customers, collecting money from them for our efforts or trading merchandise in the absence of coin—it is all the same. This is how we know we are contributing: others see the value in what we are doing and freely pay for our goods or services.

"Some earn more than others, this is true, but never will one earn everything and others earn nothing. In an open market unfettered from artificial restrictions and comprised of intelligent, creative beings, innovation of one kind or another will always bring forth viable, alternative products and support—and with them, more complimentary goods to accompany increased options. The result is an expansion of the greater economy. I rejoice at the possibilities! Those unsuited to managing their own undertakings hire themselves out to assist another person with hers. Some see more commercial success than others, without question, but everyone wins as long as they are each trying to increase worth and are willing—and able—to cover the costs of their decisions.

"A farmer who does not sell as much wheat or barley as her neighbor may still be satisfied with the quality and output of her crop. We all have distinctive levels of ambition and expectation, and of risk aversion. But if she perceives herself a failure at cultivating grain and is unwilling to improve her craft as she sees fit, then she moves on to nurturing dates or prunes or whatever else might be in demand. She may forsake farming completely and take up spinning pottery instead, or building chariots, tending young children, engineering, or shipping. A runner who cannot break into the top tier of her field might choose to compete in a different sport. I was not always a stonemason, you know. Carpentry was my earliest occupation of choice. Anyway, there are many trades for our people to pursue and an endless supply of new professions yet to be invented before the world is done.

"Fortunately, we are well-versed in the opportunities that surround us, for we have no shortage of teachers to keep us informed. I am sure we have the most creative and productive schools in the region. Parents educate their own children from a young age, and many of them continue learning outside their homes through group classes or private tutors. They might join to a master, serving for a short time as an apprentice in order to perfect their talents. After all, they must be prepared for the competitive world they will inherit, so the investment is sound.

"More mature men and women attend school as well, to learn the diverse vocations I spoke of before, or to improve existing skills, or to refine the particulars of some innovative technique. Learning is hard work to be sure and, by choice, a life-long pursuit. Who among us was born from their mother's womb a successful trader, or carpenter, or *anything*? None of us. We must all study, experiment, fall and rise, fail and push forward, devote energy to whatever we wish to develop. This is why effective instructors and coaches are valuable producers, for they multiply output through their pupils.

"The hard work of which I speak, including schoolwork, is interlaced with the other aspects of our lives—private and public. Our personalities and shared culture are integral to our economy. We learn how to act in public from our private opinions and attitudes, from the upbringing our parents provide, from the spiritual messages we accept as truth. The level of quality we place in our work and the manner in which we achieve it are significant expressions of who we are, of our independence, values, aspirations, and goals.

"We cannot afford to sacrifice our values under any circumstances—certainly not in our workplace relationships—but must consistently uphold our moral standards across all aspects of our lives. The fruits of employment belong exclusively to the person who earned them. Nobody has the right to force our labor, nor to take without our consent the private property we have gained. This includes any officials claiming authority over us, as no tax is imposed on our labors. Doing so would conflict with our ideas of competition and industry, for how tempting is it for immoral secular administrators to burden the people with unjust duties, tariffs, and fees. They are inclined to impose heavy levies to maintain extravagant lifestyles without the required exertion, or to reward their friends in iniquity, or to maintain misguided wealth redistribution schemes.

"By the same token, our judges stay out of our business interactions unless asked to resolve a conflict, refusing to give unfair advantage to one person over another because of their position, or to unduly profit from their office. Doing so would be contrary to our principles of freedom and justice. We have seen how it is the natural disposition of unchecked officials to abuse their power. Exploiting their fellow citizens in any of these ways would sap the vitality and vigor of our economy like so many leaches draining blood from prey."

Joshua paused his lecture to discern how his own students were faring. He knew he could get zealous and wanted to be sure they were not overwhelmed. They appeared to be following his speech, though it was a lot to take in at one sitting. The shadows had shortened, and his guests must be a little hungry by now, so he contemplated a change of course.

"The sun is high and I am ready to eat. Are you willing to give an old man a breather? Would you care to join me for lunch?"

"It would be our pleasure," Mahijah responded immediately, relieved to have his instructor offer a break from the discussion. He felt his mind nearly ready to explode, overloaded by everything Joshua had attempted to explain. A meal would be an appropriate occasion to relax, let the information sink in, and consider its validity.

Jubal had fared little better and was also in favor of a break, but a question lingered in his mind that he needed to ask before they indulged themselves. "Before we eat, will you explain how a people can be so happy when all they do is work? The way you describe Zion, they must do nothing else but slog along at their jobs all the time."

As soon as the words left his lips, Jubal wanted to retract his question. He remembered that Joshua had definitely mentioned the need for relaxation and leisure activities. But beyond that insight, the musician appreciated that he knew better for himself. Already he had experienced first-hand the work ethic and fondness for leisure of his adopted people, and considered it a healthy equilibrium. Lamech and his family had worked hard in the fields yesterday, and he alongside them, so he knew of their energy. They were putting in another full, demanding day at this very hour. They shared in chores at the house, managed animals and children—there was no laziness that he could perceive. And yet, they took time to enjoy each other's company, relish a good meal, and to relax in pleasing conversation with strangers wanting to learn about their society.

His own, internal answer was sufficient for the artist, but the stonemason was prone to rather exhaustive responses.

"I have heard it said that honest work is its own reward," Joshua leaned back on his cushion. "I am sure each of you have found fulfillment in a good day of labor. But humans cannot suitably sustain more than a few days—some might say hours—of all work and no play. Our focus fades and our willpower wanes. Balance in our lives is as necessary for success as it is problematic to achieve. To be sure, all professions can be difficult, strenuous, and challenging. The mind and body are not meant to work non-stop, but must be allowed to repose and rejuvenate.

"Our tradition dictates that no temporal work is to be done on the seventh day of the week. At this regular interval, we are to rest from our labors and tend to our souls. We stop all material work and devote extra time to such activities as studying from Enoch's book, personal and family praying, unselfishly serving our neighbors, and occasional fasting. This sanctified day gives us a chance to breath more easily, remember our larger obligations, and gather together with our brothers and sisters in worship. This day of rest is not a sign of laziness, but of recognition that we do not live by bread alone. It is a way to respect our God, and to ask for his blessings to be upon us.

"You have seen how hard Lamech works, and have probably considered how much effort goes into the excellent goods offered in the market. We put similar exertion into enriching hobbies and elevating distractions during all seven days of the week. Reading, writing, singing, playing games, observing the heavens, traveling throughout the countryside—you get the picture. Our side interests are as innumerable as our occupations, and sometimes the two are interchangeable. For example, I still carve stone, though not to sell to my neighbors. Obviously, I still help with repairs or small projects from time to time when a friend is in need. It gives me joy to assist in those ways. Mostly though, I pick up my tools in the cool of the evening just to see what I can create, as a decoration for the house or as a gift to my children. Others in the city work stone for a living, as I once did, but now I do it for fun. I enjoy freeing trapped creatures from the rock that encloses them, and it gives me a break from my regular duties."

"Are *we* a break from your regular duties?" Mahijah laughed, wondering to himself exactly what the stonemason did for a living now that his professional carving days were behind him.

"An interesting question. But no, you are not as relaxing as all that. In fact, *you* are my regular duties," Joshua replied with a hearty laugh of his own. "But as we discussed, work can be a joy. It undoubtedly has been for me this morning. Should we dine now? I am happy to answer any more questions you might pose while we relax over some meat."

"Do you have enough to feed unexpected guests?" Mahijah asked with concern, unwilling to unduly burden their kind host.

"Enough? Did you really ask me if there would be *enough*?" Joshua could not help but release an even bigger whoop at the notion that his table would be insufficient to feed his guests. "Dear friends, I realize there still remains much for you to learn about our Zion. Do be assured, however, that there is enough and to spare. Remind me after we eat to show you what we do with our leftovers."

"Well then, yes, we would be delighted to join you," Jubal admitted, rising with his host from the cushions and starting to shadow him into the kitchen. "I am famished. I think my appetite has grown more ravenous since we arrived in your city."

He signaled for the shepherd to follow. "But you must, gentle sir, allow us to help prepare the meal, and clean the table once we are finished. We should add our labor to support you in your errands. We would not want to be accused of idleness in the house of Joshua!"

At that remark all three friends chuckled, exiting the main room of the house to collect meat, fruit, nuts, and additional wine for their midday meal. They would need the energy it was sure to provide. Their workday was far from over.

MIGHTY LABOR
YIELDS ABUNDANCE

6

ALL THINGS IN COMMON

JUBAL WAS CURIOUS. AS HE and his friend, Mahijah, reclined on their cushions and began their feast, he wondered if every visitor to Joshua's table was treated so well. The midday meal resembled a banquet more than it did a lunch, in the extraordinary quality of nutrients as well as in the shear amount of food. There was plenty of black bread, assorted nuts, and fresh wine for him and his traveling companion, the shepherd of Sharon, to begin their meal.

Then their host, a former stonemason in Zion, brought forth the savory orange squash, a delicacy unique to the city and apparently in high demand. It was a product of innovative gardening techniques developed by Enoch, the land's chief leader. Paired with the vegetable was quail—smoked and salted and then seared in a pan just before being served. Finally, sumptuous prunes—ripe and sweet as if picked from the vine that very morning—provided a finish to the meal ... along with some goat's cheese, and a last morsel of bread, and a final cup of wine to wash everything down. One would have thought it a dying man's last supper, such as to send him with complete contentment into the netherworld.

But nobody was dying in Joshua's house today. Jubal was invigorated and buoyant beyond anything he could recall in his past—with the possible exception of yesterday. The musician of Haner and his herdsman friend had at that time enjoyed a similarly appealing if more modest lunch, and then a scrumptious and filling dinner, thanks to the kindness of a local farmer named Lamech.

Yet the meals were just an outward example of the bounty Jubal and Mahijah were feeling since they had arrived in the venerable land of Zion. It was the education and the service they experienced—the hospitality of the heart—that was convincing them little by little that they had made a good choice in visiting this ancient and enigmatic city.

As he would be harvesting dates from his farm today with his wife and children, Lamech had recommended that the visitors spend some time with Joshua instead. So far, they had not been disappointed. The travelers filled their stomachs *well* before the presented fare could be depleted.

"Look, my friends. I see that our food has outlasted our appetites. Very good! Let us talk some more, for there is much left for me to relate regarding the principles of Zion. But before your next questions, please tell me your history prior to encountering Enoch. I seek the pleasure of knowing you better. Take as long as you like."

Joshua had spent the latter half of the morning in conversation with his visitors, but so intrigued had they been to learn of his city as they began to talk, that he immediately indulged them rather than hearing more detailed information about their identity and purpose. It mattered little, for the retired stonemason was happy to accept them into his house as they were, in advance of an informed judgement. So before lunch, he expounded on the financial principles behind the wealth of his people, the righteous citizens of Zion who were rejecting the sadness and scarcity of their neighboring lands and making each other wealthy beyond measure.

With their noontime meal completed, and as Joshua was in no hurry, the visitors accommodated his invitation, revealing their peculiar backgrounds in turn and their common, newfound aspiration to discover lasting happiness.

Jubal had grown up in a happy if modest home, the son of a carpenter and brother of two girls. His mother formed their small residence into a warm and pleasant one, with kind words and what tasty treats their limited income could afford. His father taught him to be honest and hard-working while exposing him to the delights and distresses of life in the city. The patriarch carved him a flute of nine pipes, and it was in the marketplace at his father's side that Jubal refined his skill. The boy became so adept that he quit the home of his parents earlier than expected in order to earn a fortune with his music, a strategy that did not last long.

Married but childless, his wealth was already gone when Haner was viciously attacked, besieged, and then ruined. Burdened by their new masters with a perpetual tribute of twenty percent on all they might possess or acquire, the conquered population was allowed to return to their former dwellings. But his house was empty, his wife missing—presumed enslaved—and his parents and siblings killed. Still a young man, Jubal all but renounced the one surviving source of joy in his life—his custom-made flute. It was not until later that he chanced upon his cloak-making friend in the streets of his wrecked city.

Mahijah's life had also been one of sadness. He was born in the neighboring land of Sharon, where famine and betrayal highlighted most of his life among the sheep. He learned at an early age to sew, becoming well-practiced at the craft, but could find satisfaction in neither his profession nor his personal life. He relocated to Haner after the death of his wife and children to start over on the vacated land of another shepherding family, slaughtered during the recent war. It was in the streets of that city, still recovering from the invasion, that he encountered Jubal. They became companions, sharing with each other their complaints of former woes. Despite past trials, the old man would not completely abandon his hope for a better life, and tried to buoy up his younger friend, though mostly to no avail.

The reality was that the pilgrims' stories were quite typical. The histories of their nations—even back before they were organized and recognizable as such—had been full of conflict, distress, and grief. Such is the fate of every person to some degree, the nature of our existence being a fallen and a mortal one, packed with pain and agony, bound to end in death. The rain falls, the wind blows, and the sun shines—all oblivious to our consent. Wars rage, economies collapse, crops fail, robbers conspire, and jealousies and greed move the weak, desperate, and downright evil to inflict hurt and horror.

As we examine our lives, it is evident that there is very little of the world about us that is in our control except for the most important thing of all: our free will. Amid exposure to harsh elements and the vices of mankind, we admit that we do in fact have tremendous influence over our own decisions—perhaps completely so. We find that we are corrupt men and women, prompted to be good, trying to be better, stumbling much of the time. Our inherited world is designed to test our mettle against unique and significant challenges, at times almost more than we can bear. Little wonder we tend to misstep, give up, and give in to the baser natures of our existence. It would be more surprising if the opposite were true.

Which was exactly what made Zion exceptional. From its fertile fields and prosperous pastures outside the city, past its formidable walls and gates, and into the homes of its free and purposeful people, the revered City of Holiness was different. Substantially absent from its society were the strife and sadness so prevalent in the outside world. Its unassuming opulence was unaffected by the capriciousness of weather or the threats of an enemy. This was not so because the occupants of Zion were more or less than human, but because they had learned to make small and steady improvements in their behaviors through regular, good choices, and to reap the related rewards.

Zion's residents followed the divine principles imparted by Enoch, their prophet. They were joined in common cause to seek an elevated ethic. In living by these precepts, they thrived, gathering themselves and their possessions safely within their fortified righteousness—the great walls of their city being symbols of a superior, inner strength. They were applying their moral agency to serve each other in charity. They were happy.

By chance it seemed, scarcely more than a week ago, Jubal and Mahijah had learned that Enoch, the seer, was preaching in the land of Haner on a hill outside its city's western gate. The friends sought him out, listened to his instruction, asked clarifying questions, and then resolved to follow his advice and seek Zion for themselves. Their journey required six days of arduous travel through the desert, with them arriving in the land on the seventh. Their only expectation was to observe the city and its inhabitants, not to be welcomed so openly by its residents, nor to partake so generously of their joy.

"The lower our lows, the higher our highs. My soul is gladdened that you have persevered and joined us these last days, at least for a short time," the stonemason said, accepting their stories without question. He understood that the hardships of their lives were as valid and real as any he had so far heard, or that he would later hear, while seated at his table.

"Your adventure to our land reminds me of one of our greatest challenges. Our older children who have grown up in the city have not lived through many of the dire struggles you describe. It is hard for them to fathom the difficulty of life outside Zion, and therefore to appreciate the bounty in body and spirit that we enjoy. For this reason, we encourage them, once they have reached a level of maturity, to travel about the area and acquaint themselves with foreign customs and practices. Many of them follow this counsel and explore the realms outside our walls, returning to recount their tales from afar.

"We are all enriched by this practice. It is exciting to hear of diverse perspectives, yet heartbreaking to be reminded of the anguish surrounding us. A large number of our offspring, even those who have toured the world, become unsatisfied with the teachings of their childhood and decide to reject Zion, preferring to live after a contrary manner. Either they are more attracted to the cultures and habits of the external world, or they are tricked into thinking there is happiness in worshipping other gods, or they simply rebel against the generations of their elders as youth are want to do. A single lost child is already too many, but we must respect their individual liberty.

"And yet, despite our losses, our numbers slowly swell. We divide our congregations so that we are better able to know and serve each other. Still, before long our substance will be too great, and we will not all be able to dwell together. There has already been talk of establishing a second city—a colony of Zion, so to speak—in a location beyond our walls a short distance to the south."

Jubal, full from his meal and ready to continue their earlier conversation, eased them back into it. "Speaking of enrichment, this morning you explained that laboring with your might was the secret to Zion's noticeably-impressive, economic success. But while everyone appears to be well-fed, healthy, and satisfied, we have not witnessed any of your upper class."

Mahijah nudged his younger companion with his elbow, giving him a silent glare from the corner of the low table. Turning to look at the center of the slab, Jubal noticed the same, small sack of coins that their host had set down earlier that morning and where it remained untouched. Naamah, the young daughter of Lamech, the farmer, had given the purse to Joshua at his front door. Its delivery had been the last part of her assignment to escort her adopted uncles to his house before leaving to help her family harvest the last of their dates in the fields to the north of the city.

The flute player blushed as he seized on the reason for his companion's knock. Flustered, he managed to speak an apology, saying, "Oh, I did not mean—please do not misunderstand. Your house and clothing and the fare of your table are as fine as any we have seen in the city. Perhaps *you* are a member of the upper class?"

If the retired stonemason were to be offended, it would take much more effort than Jubal's naïve slip. Without hesitation, he responded, "I hardly think so. If that were the case, you would have seen indications in our streets of a lower class—people suffering or lacking, to some degree, that which they needed or wanted. Was that your experience?"

The shepherd made as if to answer in his place, but Joshua motioned for him to allow their young friend to respond. Jubal took a moment to give the question its due reflection.

"Well, now that you mention it, I do not suppose that is the case at all. Lamech and his family are farmers, and their house and table are as lovely as your own, though dissimilar in many respects. They appeared to lack nothing while we were in their care, but neither did they boast on account of any superfluous possession. Everyone we have seen in the streets—from outward appearances—has been well-nourished, at ease, abundantly clothed, and untroubled. There has been nobody begging, nor petitioning unduly, nor idle for that matter. What I mean to say is that we have noticed neither obvious lacking nor blatant extravagance among Zion's inhabitants. No flamboyant robes nor excessive purchases, no gilded litters nor unnecessary servants, no overindulgences of any kind."

"I *have* noticed, however, and with great pleasure," Mahijah the cloak maker could not resist making his point, "that the clothing your people wear is well-constructed, with master needlework and impressive decorations. Truly of remarkable quality. With guidance and practice, I might someday create their equal. Still, we witnessed nothing brazen. Elegant is the word I would use to describe it, though every person carries such a distinction about her, including yourself."

"You are both discerning. Thank you for your praises," Joshua replied, satisfied with their responses. "The reason you have missed any class distinction is because there is none. We are all the same, of one social class. We do not admire a person because of their possessions, but because of who they are. Just like our judges are no respecter of persons, so the rest of us esteem each man our brother, each woman our sister. We recognize each other for the priceless, inimitable individuals that we are, and support our inhabitants in becoming better and happier. Such is the proper purpose of wealth: to serve others.

"We love our people, not our money. There is no benefit in one person having more at the expense of her fellow resident. Of course, we congratulate and respect efforts to create wealth, but not the silver and gold itself. Nothing good springs from the worship of such idols. You may trust me in this, for I know well the consequences of such false devotion."

"I regret having gained some of that knowledge myself, through my own sad experience of days not far past. But does this imply that you limit the amount that a person can earn, or take from them their excess? I thought liberty was the foundational principle of your success." Jubal was trying to comprehend.

"Your understanding of our individual independence is accurate.

Nobody is justified in taking from you, by force or without permission, something that is properly yours. They cannot break into your house, hijack your table, and demand of your meat and bread. That would violate your liberty and property, not to mention your privacy and personal space. What motivation would there be for you to learn a craft such as stone carving, expend huge energies to fashion a fine piece, then bargain with your customers in the marketplace to sell it, only for some ill-advised magistrate to take from you its fair price in coin at the edge of a sword? No. Your desire to work would then be immediately crippled, and our prosperity as a society would plummet overnight. The sanctity of liberty insists that we respect the private property rights of our neighbors.

"We are each private citizens, free to pursue our livelihoods as we see fit. The only limits to our commercial success are self-imposed. This house, its furnishings—my wardrobe, tools, lands, and animals—all are mine to use. They are my delight and my responsibility. I employ them to meet the needs and wants of my household, and maintain them so that they might add to my happiness. I am the captain of what silver and gold is in my possession, and it serves me well."

"Ah, I think I grasp your implication. So instead of flaunting their excess, the residents of Zion save their silver and gold, securing them under lock and key for future purchases or calamities. There must be chests overflowing with riches in houses throughout the city!" Jubal nearly shouted, reminded for an instant of his own past wealth and the envy it had provoked. His eyes lit up as he reflected on the passions he had gratified with that wasted money.

"You are correct that we do not boast in our surplus, but not for the reason you describe. I know of no family in our land that stashes silver or gold at their residence. They serve their God and each other through diligent, intelligent hard work, but do not rely on themselves for relief in times of want. I have read about such days in our distant past, but have not lived through any such time myself, despite my many years. Self-reliance borders on the sin of pride. Yes, we work independently and are accountable for our own actions, but we put our full trust in the principles that we have repeatedly proven to be sound, given us by our God. It is he, after all, who commands us to work, and we have faith in his commands.

"We do keep supplies on hand for our immediate needs, and food must obviously be stored for the winter. You must have seen the silos and barns in our pastures as you approached the city, holding grain until it can be ground or fruits until they can be preserved. Even so, we stand disposed to help a neighbor as necessary. It is better to give today to those of our public who are in need, than to watch them go hungry or naked while we hoard for our private tomorrows."

Mahijah became a little self-conscious. Just about everyone he had met in the city looked young, or at least younger than expected. The grayed herdsman wondered exactly how old Joshua could be. The stonemason was undoubtedly among the seniors of the land, but he did not appear overly wrinkled, or physically feeble, or mentally inhibited by his years. Their host was more ancient than Lamech, to be sure, but probably not by much. Mahijah worried that everybody he met in Zion must think him to be older than dirt itself!

"Do you remember Lamech speaking to you yesterday afternoon of a shared purpose among all our people? And later that evening, he told you—did he not—of the common goals that we share to be moral and act according to the teachings we have received? We should each have private motivations and personal goals. And yet, how much more powerful can they be when aligned with a unified vision and shared objectives.

"This is what we do with our surplus," Joshua illustrated as he reached across the low table for the bag of coins delivered earlier in the morning by Naamah. He loosened the sack to briefly peer inside and note that the coins were silver, then tied the string tightly, not giving himself enough time to count the contents. He then pushed it across the table to rest in front of Jubal.

"As soon as we have more than we need, when our wants are filled and we still have excess from our profitmaking endeavors, we donate it to our inspired stewards. Large or small—it matters not—we deposit our economic leftovers into the only type of bank or savings establishment extant in all of the city: the storehouse of God. It is there that coinage, tools, clothing, furniture, raw materials, salted meats, fruits sealed in jars, livestock, books, toys—everything you can think of that is useful for our survival and development—is organized and preserved for the benefit of all. Goods of every kind are offered freely—willingly—by those who have them to contribute.

"Occasionally, goods and gold are even given by neighbors who must sacrifice to do so, but that is not typical. Those who are unable to donate because they have nothing extra, why, they give nothing, of course. And if there are some who have suffered setbacks—like bad luck or illness, accidents or poor judgement, maybe a short spell of idleness—they are made whole from our abundance in the warehouse. Regardless, the storehouse belongs to us all. It is a public hedge against any disaster. We sleep soundly knowing all is safely gathered in, that there is enough and to spare. We have all things in common."

The friends leaned back on their cushions, stunned by the stonemason's explanation. They had both become convinced that every man, woman, and child was possessor and heir to enormous fortunes. But now they were being told—as they supposed—that nobody in the city owned more than the basics which they needed to survive. Joshua must have contradicted himself. He had proclaimed in one breath that his people submitted to no taxes, but with his next had confessed that they surrendered to their civic rulers everything which they could not use individually or in their families. It was a paradox that the guests could not immediately resolve.

The stonemason nibbled on an almond, amused at the obvious frustration in his friends' eyes.

"Did you not tell us this very morning that there were no taxes in Zion?" Jubal asked. "What you have described resembles a *massive* tax, greater than the tribute required of us by our Heni overlords."

Jubal was referring to the ferocious nation which had conquered his homeland, killing many and enslaving the rest. The outcasts of Haner had been allowed to return to their city, but were forced to pay tribute in the amount of a fifth of all they possessed. It was a grievous affliction.

"I am pleased that you have been listening," Joshua retorted, unrepentant of his previous words. "That is correct: we have no tax. Our excess is not granted to government officials, but to the private cooperative of our inhabitants who are members of their specific storehouse. We essentially take of our private surplus and grant it to everyone in the section of the city in which we live, through the administration of our resident priest attached to the local warehouse. Our people are privileged to contribute all of their surplus goods and services at their own behest. They are not obligated to be charitable, for that would be the same as theft. To their credit, they are so committed to this principle that they have made a covenant to follow it.

"Our magistrates only receive money for their time sitting in judgement, a small amount if they accept it at all. They accumulate no tributes nor fees to create personal largess and burdens over our residents, no bribes to corrupt their decrees. This part of our financial system may be unlike any you have experienced. Our inhabitants donate the extra that they earn from their labors—of their own accord—for their mutual advantage, and not for the expenses of the judges. No force is employed, for it is neither necessary nor permitted.

"I am one of their priests and help them stay true to their covenant. With my two advisors, and according to divine will, I hold our collective goods safe for the use of all. Plus, as it becomes needed, I divide inheritances and property among those living in my part of the city, counseling together with each individual and family in private conference how they wish to serve our community and be served by it. My clerk keeps meticulous records in these matters so that there is no question about what commitments have been made. We are a record-keeping people."

Mahijah was taken aback, speaking in disbelief, "Yours is a unique system of preserving wealth, though it matches the unity of Zion found in other aspects of your culture, which we have studied under Enoch and Lamech. If the residents of a society were to share in a desire to be happy, live by the same moral standards, and work for the common good, why would it be unusual for them to pool their monetary resources? However, what if someone decided to not participate in your covenant, or to break it once she entered into it?"

"It is quite simple really," said Joshua with a matter-of-fact tone. "Visitors come and go as they please. Nobody would dare to trap them in our city against their will. Let us suppose that a visitor decides to remain in Zion as one of our people, a choice she would freely make with full knowledge of our beliefs and practices. She would come before the priest geographically located nearest to where she planned to take a house, and openly pledge to follow our principles. She would then demonstrate her commitment for a short season while living among us. Once her promise had been publicly confirmed, she would then give everything she owned to the storehouse."

"*Everything?*" Jubal interrupted in astonishment.

"Everything," Joshua confirmed with decisiveness.

"In giving it to the priest, she is actually giving it to God, recognizing his ownership over the whole world and her small morsel of its bounty. She and the priest then jointly decide what she will need to support her family and perform her labors. Clothing, housing, tools, livestock, education—every last concern is considered. She is provided with means in proportion to her responsibilities and becomes the sole agent of those goods. For a young and growing family, or for interests requiring much capital, she will need a larger portion. But for a smaller and aging family, or for a more straightforward vocation, she will require a smaller allotment. They invoke our Maker to sense his approval in their decisions and she becomes a steward over that portion of God's property within her care.

"Not just that, but she also must have enough resources for reasonable desires and hobbies beyond the basic necessities. Did I mention this morning that we do not live by bread alone? Orange squash and seared quail cannot be passed by if we are to enjoy life to its fullest! Nor can we ignore the noble enticements of music, art, and other virtuous distractions or forms of expression. The clerk chronicles her inheritance so that nothing is mistaken when she comes next before the priest to make an accounting or to ask for aid.

"And then, off to work she goes, earning by the sweat of her brow all that she can honestly produce in the free market. If she cannot make ends meet, then she gets more help from our collective stores until she can at least break even. When once a surplus of her wants and needs is produced, she immediately gives it all to the priest. Every extra garment, every unused tool or toy, every spare coin. Why keep something you do not need or want? Useless clutter borders on selfishness. Our dwellings tend to be neat and orderly, in part because we simply give away—for someone else to use—anything we no longer require nor desire. The priest checks in with the steward now and again as the spirit moves him—every few years or so in my experience—to make sure all needs are being met. As her family situation fluctuates over time, she will donate fewer or further of her goods, but her offering will be constantly equivalent for her. She will always contribute out of her excess, so as to never create a scarcity.

"If ever something in her life changes and she wishes to leave the city, or if she decides to break the covenant, she is free to do so. There is no crime in it so the magistrate is not involved at all. It is, however, a transgression against God, and consequences—ever tempered by as much mercy as can be proffered—must follow. She must give up all that she managed under her stewardship and rely on her own efforts from that time forward to survive, as when she first freely contracted with her oath.

"I have witnessed both ends of this very occurrence. Few who break the covenant stay in the city. Why would they? If someone prefers to no longer live according to God's will, or is uncomfortable with our culture, she merely moves to another nation whose habits suit her better—frequently with supplies dispersed from our stores to ease her journey. The details of each case vary according to specific needs, but in general, Zion cannot be governed by hearts and minds under duress. It is only through persuasion and loving kindness, fair discipline and quick forgiveness, that it can be directed. We do employ servants from time to time, but we cannot endure slavery. And if anyone who has broken their promise in Zion turns about and genuinely longs to renew it, or to return to the city, she is again welcomed as at the beginning and takes the pledge once more."

"Is there no debt to be repaid for someone who abandons your borders?" Mahijah thought aloud. "With all that is given, it seems that only the rapidly rich would break such a promise, possessing greater than they could want. And only the perpetually poor would rely on it to fill their bellies, wishing to avoid the responsibilities of work."

"No, we incur no monetary debts, nor hold any over a brother's head, for are we not all beggars?" the stonemason explained. He was accustomed to explaining these principles as part of his priestly duties, and found gratification in vocalizing them to novices in the ways of Zion. "That would betray gross ingratitude on our part, and we strive to be thankful in all things. I have heard that some in other lands charge interest of their friends, but no such practice exists among our people. Some few have tried to abuse our covenants—the dishonest hoarding riches or sneaking away in the night with them, or the idle forgetting their duty to contribute—but such deviations are infrequent and temporary, and we immediately correct them in view of helping the misguided."

"Well then, what if someone insists on continuing in a field of labor that does not thrive? Will she always be receiving help instead of giving it?" Mahijah could muster at least one more question for the priest.

"Out of the storehouse, we invest in new initiatives and help struggling ones through tough times. Rarely, if ever, do we try to shore up an underperforming enterprise that is failing due to lack of demand. The free market reveals what we as a people desire to consume and what is of little worth. Low quality items, or outdated technology, or untasteful foodstuffs are not purchased, and eventually their proprietors cannot earn enough money to survive. If someone does not correct such a course on her own, the local priest will naturally give her assistance to get by, but will also counsel her on what changes she can make to become a contributor once more. Maybe working harder or updating her processes is all that is needed, or more education, or a different profession entirely."

While outside the heat of the afternoon was increasing, the friends were still cool inside the priest's abode, the windows open to allow a soft breeze into the chamber. Jubal was relaxed and comfortable enough to continue his questioning.

"What of the walls and gates and other substantial works throughout the city? If everyone is giving away their excess, and there are no public taxes, how does anyone have money to build such large edifices? They must take a lot of gold to construct."

"They do indeed," replied Joshua. "The walls and other structures are built from the same storehouse funds we have been discussing. When a possible community improvement is identified, it is discussed among the people and the priests. This is our city and our land—after all—and we all have a joint concern in making it the best it can be. They provide arguments for the project, consider opinions against it, and the priests closest to the project make a decision. If they are inclined to proceed, monies are entrusted to a temporary steward for the project and work begins. Everyone cooperates to make the common effort prosperous. Individuals may be employed to assist in the action, or will volunteer their labor and materials. Depending on the development, we might hire someone to maintain it once completed, or to schedule its usage so that all is in order and to ensure we can all take full advantage of it. Such was our approach with the marketplace you have already visited. Careful records are kept to make sure we are being wise agents over our joint assets, which are really God's assets. At the close of the project, any unexploited funds are returned. We usually have a celebration of some sort as well. As you will remember, all work and no play …"

Joshua had not slowed down since their noontime break to eat, and now sensed that his students could use a breather. He would not object to the idea, either.

"And on that topic, play *may* be in order for the three of us right about now. It is hard work sitting on plush cushions, bending our stubborn minds around new concepts. I think you might very well enjoy a visit to the storehouse. It is just outside, adjacent to my dwelling. Would you like to see it?"

"Yes, of course!" The flute player was on his feet in an instant, ignoring the light sarcasm. He impatiently waited as his older friends rose and stretched their limbs.

Joshua grabbed Naamah's purse from the table, then took the lead through his front door and into the open air. The sun shone brilliantly along its path to the west, not a cloud to be seen in the blue sky. The priest immediately turned to walk through the empty courtyard that was in front of the three large, cubed structures adjacent to his residence. The center building bore a large door like a barn, wide enough to allow steers to enter four abreast, while the two buildings on the sides showed smaller doors like a typical house, only large enough for a man. There was no sign of any other workers or assistants about the courtyard, and only the soft lowing of cattle could be heard from behind the three doors.

This was the storehouse of Zion? The musician was confused. There must be tremendous wealth inside, and yet there were no exterior guards to prevent theft. As Joshua led them past the nearest doors and towards the one furthest away, he saw no bolts or locks to prevent unwanted entry, just simple latches to keep the wind from blowing them open. They entered the most distant cube of the structure.

Joshua walked inside first, followed by his students. Once his eyes adjusted to the dimness of the interior, Jubal became convinced that he could now die at peace, having seen everything there was to see in the mortal world. Within the building, aisles upon aisles of horizontally-laid timbers stretched to the ceiling and extended to the back wall, shelves containing all the materials Joshua had described to them while back in his habitation. Above ground level were stacked tools and cut lumber, chairs and tables, bedding and cloth, water jugs and foodstuffs—everything a family might need to survive. He noticed a collection of musical instruments: a harp and several lyres, some drums with a construction he could not recognize. There were too many types of assets for the friends to distinguish. On the floor were a number of chests, closed and latched—but again, unlocked—of various sizes and shapes. All was in good order, with no debris to block the aisles, nor refuse to spoil the cleanliness.

Joshua moved over to the chest closest to the door, twisted the latch that held it shut, and opened it without hesitation, his guests stringing along behind him like children eager to see the unveiling of something new. The trunk was filled to the top with silver and gold coins almost to overflowing. Joshua lifted the sack and untied the string keeping it sealed, turned it upside down, and unceremoniously dumped the money into the chest, careful to aim for the center of the stash so as not to spill any on the floor. He closed the lid, then took the empty purse and tossed it into a basket stationed at the head of the aisle, full of other sacks like Naamah's.

"Looks like we need to start another chest," he mumbled, "or give away more money!" He laughed out loud as if remembering a private joke shared previously with good friends, slapping Jubal on the back before making for the exit. All of the unopened trunks were assuredly filled to a similar level with precious stones and metals.

"Please look around for as long as you like. You can access the other two buildings through connecting doors, but they are essentially the same as this one. We do keep watch over some cattle, sheep, goats, pigs, and other livestock, though all save a few sick beasts are currently in the fields being tended by trusted volunteers. We can walk out to see them, too, if the mood moves you. I will wait for you outside in the sun."

"Will you not count the money? How do you know the extent of Lamech's contribution?" Jubal was still flustered by the immeasurable riches before him in the building, just one-third of the total under Joshua's purview. He was more shocked at the trust Joshua placed in his donators. But admittedly, his greatest amazement was the confidence the priest seemed to place in two strangers from a foreign land who had just toured the most splendid accumulation of riches in the region, and been left alone to examine them.

Joshua stopped to answer. "No, we never do. Why would we bother? Whether a sack bulging with gold or a widow's mite, it is all the same. No logs are kept of what donors put in, for it all belongs to Zion, to our God. We each depart this storehouse the same, with everything which we could need and want, but nothing more. You might think I am the richest man in the land, for all this is under my care. But you would be dead wrong. I am just as rich as everyone else—equally so. None of this here is mine, except for the small house I have used to entertain you today. No, like my old friend, Enoch, sometimes likes to say, I am the poorest man in Zion and happy to be so. I would wish it no other way."

The priest exited the building, its door swinging shut behind him, leaving Jubal and Mahijah in relative darkness compared to the brightness outside. They could hear the old stonemason shout a greeting to someone in the courtyard, mention something about rain, then engage in an indistinct conversation sprinkled with laughter. It must have been someone he knew. Was there anyone in the city he did not?

The travelers lingered behind to gaze at the treasure. It was as large as a king's ransom—ransoms for three kings, if all be counted. Jubal was obligated to confess that with all of this treasure at the disposal of the *least* among the people in the city, she would be demonstrably richer than the richest man in the wealthiest city in the world.

Most of the surplus was amassed on wooden racks and ledges beyond their reach. The uncles looked at each other, then at the chest of silver and gold that was most seductively within their reach, and plainly out of sight of their host. Jubal stretched for the lid, unlatched it, and raised it with one hand.

Mahijah was curious but not alarmed by his friend's actions. Back in Haner, the shepherd was regularly concerned about what his friend might do. But that was a lifetime ago, a painful memory that grew dimmer with each hour they spent in this place, with each discussion they held among its residents. The herdsman was different now, almost a new person, and he could tell from his friend's conversation and demeanor that Jubal had changed, too. Their attitudes, expectations, desires—everything was altered for the better. They were happier than he remembered either of them ever being in their former land. It was like a gorgeous dream from which he was loathe to awaken. He wondered if he ever would.

Jubal reached at his waist with his other hand. For all the intensity of Naamah's hugging, his coin purse had not been shaken from its place.

It had secreted only sand for the last two years, though now it jingled with the sound of four silver coins, earned that very morning in the marketplace, tokens of appreciation for his talent with the flute.

He untied the knot that held the bag secure, then upended it above the center of the chest as Joshua had done. His falling coins caused less of a stir in the trunk than had Naamah's, but no less of an impact.

"That was all the money in my possession," he told his friend, tears welling in his eyes. He reverently laid down the lid, latched it in place, and walked towards the door, leaving the storehouse as rich as everyone else who was blessed to pass through its confines. Outside, a blazing sun awaited his moist face.

SURPLUS CREATES SHARED SAVINGS

7

No Poor Among Them

JUBAL WAS PLEASED AS HE let the desert sun beat down on his face. After passing most of the morning and the early afternoon in the coolness of Joshua's house, he was happy for the warmth he now felt on his skin—though it was nothing to compare with the warmth in his heart. Jubal, the flute player of Haner, had been a guest in the majestic City of Zion for barely two days, and already he felt like one of its residents. This sentiment transcended the welcome and kindness he received from the owner of the house, the aged but still vibrant priest and former stonemason, in whose courtyard he stood.

Along with his traveling companion, Mahijah, the former shepherd of Sharon, he had been graciously received the day before by Lamech, a farmer of the land. The dark-haired cultivator of crops invited them to work in his fields with his family, provided dinner and bed for the night at his house in the city, and offered his daughter to be their escort to the priest's dwelling the next morning. As they walked to meet the priest at the start of the day, they were routinely greeted as friends by complete strangers in the city streets and enjoyed the marketplace as if they were full-fledged citizens. Jubal even earned a little silver as a guest flutist.

But that was not the joy Jubal contemplated. He was beginning to accept the teachings he received from these people and to act upon them. The whole adventure had started with a happy circumstance back in Haner eight days ago, when Mahijah, his companion, convinced him to listen to a wild man preaching outside their city. The gray shepherd and cloak maker felt a burning desire to listen to the wandering evangelist, positive that the seer could light the path to some durable happiness. He brought Jubal along with him to the small hill west of the city gate. That encounter prompted both men to journey to Zion, listening first to Lamech, and then to Joshua in turn as they expanded upon the principles that their people daily embraced to attain lifelong joy.

Just minutes ago, he had submitted all the money he possessed in the world—money he had earned barely hours earlier by playing a borrowed pan flute—to the common storehouse of God, which was in the care of his host. With those four donated pieces of silver, he made a personal pledge to join with the inhabitants of Zion whom he hardly knew, but dearly loved.

Mahijah had witnessed Jubal's selfless gift and understood the significance of his charitable act, but was not taken aback by it. He, too, sensed the unmistakable attraction for living in this land with its occupants. He understood that here his young friend could continue his work as a musician, construct a new and grander flute of many pipes to replace his current one, and earn an honest living playing for the buyers and sellers in the bazaar. For himself, the herdsman could also keep sheep and sew cloaks for customers as he had done in his former lands, though with the freedom requisite to expand his holdings and perfect his skill. All this work they would both perform surrounded by a free people joined in a quest for joy, dedicated to doing what they thought was virtuous, and taking the cares of their neighbors upon their own shoulders.

Mahijah made the same silent decision his friend had made, and determined to be a future shepherd and merchant of Zion.

Looking back on a lifetime of desolation, Mahijah was a little astonished at how difficult the decision was for him. Perhaps the miserable momentum of his nearly one hundred years was the explanation. After so much suffering and sadness, he had become accustomed to the nature of his existence and was reluctant to try something different. Such is the character of man, that change is so distressing, the fear of the unfamiliar so fierce, that we would rather persist in the wretchedness we know than risk a more excellent way by altering our course through a foreign setting.

As a less aged man, Mahijah had heard about Zion, the terrible city occupied by devils with red eyes and horns extending from their heads, whose sole amusement was to inflict pain and suffering on their enemies. At least that was one version of the legends in his memory. Equally possible were the contrary stories that warmed a cold heart, describing a peaceful land of harmony and plenty with only health and gladness, and streets lined with gold. He never determined which if any of the accounts were accurate—never gave much attention to the unreliable whispers—but his soul leaped with hopefulness when he heard the name Zion shouted in the streets of Haner. Maybe his life was not as sad as he imagined, or maybe the duty he felt for his young friend's welfare inspired him with boldness. In any event, he made the six-day strenuous trek through the wilderness to his desired destination with his partner in tow, and stayed open to the influence of its teachers.

He did not regret his choice.

From the courtyard, Mahijah turned himself about to shut and latch the door he and Jubal had just exited, chortling at the notion that there was no need for a lock on it. In the cube-shaped warehouse they had just toured at its keeper's invitation, there was silver and gold—durable goods and preserved perishables—enough to satisfy the kings of three plenteous nations. And yet, there were no fences to block the way, no guards to detain trespassers, no keyed bolts to frustrate the tempted. As he turned to join his stoic friend in the sunlight, he smiled and shook his head—like a person who has discovered something too good to be true and yet pictures no reasonable option but to accept it. How could he disbelieve his own eyes? He walked up behind Jubal, rested his hand on the artist's shoulder for a few seconds, and then left him to continue walking towards the dusty corner of the courtyard. The younger man caught up to him as he reached it.

Mahijah took a seat on the bench abutting the barrier, favoring a bit of shade that fell across its wooden planks. Jubal remained erect, standing comfortably beside him in the full sun, soaking in its rays as he reviewed in his mind all he had learned these last days. The travelers said nothing between themselves while waiting, for they did not need to speak a word. By now, they entirely realized the harmony they shared in longing to become one with their new friends in Zion.

The priest finished his jovial conversation with the middle-aged woman who had stopped by his residence, then noticed his two new brothers resting by the wall adjacent to the most distant of the three cubed structures. He walked towards them.

"That was one of our neighbors," Joshua pointed over his shoulder with a shout, strolling to the bench and taking a seat next to the shepherd. "She is always finding ways to help with my duties. Who am I fooling? Our neighbors all contribute to my work, practically doing it for me. What would I do without them? Now, I see that you have returned the latch on the exterior door for me. My thanks to you. What did you think of our humble storehouse?"

The storehouse, three cubical buildings adjacent to Joshua's personal residence, contained a portion of the shared wealth of this great city. It was stocked full of treasure, goods and gold—the common surplus of the occupants of Zion—and managed by the priest in this area of the city. It was an immeasurable fortune. Before lunch, Joshua had been explaining to his two guests the principle of having all things in common, completing a brief tour of the facility before speaking with the woman in the courtyard. His stamina had not waned then, and he was apparently ready to continue their conversation now.

"We have no words," Mahijah answered.

"I see," came the reply.

Joshua was neither surprised by the look in the traveler's faces, nor dismayed by their silence. On the contrary, he seemed motivated to teach them more about the affluence of his land, and how his people managed their financial affairs.

"Though I cannot know for sure, I dare say we have the greatest financial wealth in all the world. It seems from your reaction that you both would concur. The resources in this and the other storehouses throughout the city represent the hard work, generosity, and faithfulness of our men and women. We take the command to be industrious seriously, and each person who contributes to this accumulation is first supporting herself, making individual choices about what to produce and what to purchase.

"Did you notice the variety and quality of the goods inside? Those are the *extra* items, the leftovers when all needs and wants have been covered. We do not compete with our neighbors in displaying our excess, for what value is there in such vanity? Instead, we add it to our collective savings, store it away for the mutual benefit, whether it be a prospective improvement to our city or as a hedge against some future disaster. In this purpose, as in so many others, we are one."

"The question on my mind might be presumptuous of me, but I'll ask it anyway. Is it possible that someday my friend and I might contribute to your affluence?" Mahijah questioned while looking Joshua directly in the eyes, a genuine yearning blossoming in his own. "We have little to offer, no property or connections of which to speak. My hands grow weak and tired, with not many years of use left within them, I am afraid. But our hearts are willing, are they not, Jubal?"

The musician, leaning against the wall and bending over at his waist, nodded silently, his eyes fixed on the sand at his feet, his fingers caressing the flute of former years, which he still protected in the folds of his cloak.

"Have you not already contributed," Joshua asked solemnly, breaking from Mahijah's gaze to motion with his head at the flute player.

Jubal looked up from the ground with a jolt and turned towards the bench to stare at his host in unbelief. He then glared at the shepherd, who shrugged his shoulders and held his palms up to show he was unaware of how the priest could have known about the four silver coins. Like Enoch the seer, the priest's perception benefited from celestial assistance.

Joshua ignored their reaction, sighed deeply and looked at the sky. "You see, it takes more than words or good intentions to find lasting happiness. It takes action. Otherwise, what need would there have been for us to be clothed in mortal bodies and placed on this earth? We could have professed our love for God and our desire to be like him while cradled in the sanctuary of our heavenly home. Our spirits may be willing, but in the weakness of our human flesh we establish the authenticity of our declarations. We are here as fallen and carnal beings to test the width, height, and depth—the very ends—of our love. We require bodies of blood and bone to prove, by our behavior, the truthfulness we assert to be within our hearts and minds."

The priest rose from his seat and offered Jubal his former place on the bench, waiting for the artist to take it before picking up his lecture, standing before his audience. "In the great wide world, there is little patience and less compassion. The strong attack the weak, the bold mock the meek, and the learned-proud shame the ignorant and humble. Kings abuse their subjects, enforcing their whimsical wills with soldier and sword, demanding tribute whether their people can survive without it or not.

"But things are not so in Zion. Here, the strong protect the weak, coaching them to increase in strength. The bold commend the timid, inspiring them to add courage to their submissiveness. Within our walls, the educated glory in sharing their knowledge, using it to lift and bless others and to give thanks to God.

"As you recall, we rule ourselves unfettered from the corruption of a mortal king, instead acting under the direction of our heavenly, steadfast sovereign. We are forced to pay no earthly tribute, no unwieldy taxes, yet we freely sacrifice our time, talents, and possessions. Diligent effort is what our God requires of us, and what we ask of each other. We only have mastery over ourselves, and so can only be expected to do what is within our power. Every person who puts forth sound effort, hard work in her proper domain, can be assured of a place with us. If you in humility accept our principles and are willing to try your hand at joining us, we will place no obstacles in your way. On the contrary, we will support you until you succeed."

"But what if I am not able to work? As I said, I have lost much of my manual dexterity. Neither do my eyes see as well as they once did. My soul might be disposed to help, but my body more and more frequently shrinks from heavy loads. It is likely that my mind will fail me at some point as well," Mahijah bemoaned the aches and pains of aging, and Joshua stepped closer to place an understanding hand on his shoulder.

"You are correct, wise one. The Lord and his people make up the difference for us, after all we can do. We are each expected to give as much as we can—everything really—to the cause of Zion. For those beyond their prime, the nature of that effort will evolve to accommodate their individual situations. Some with the capacity and the desire to continue earning a living will shift careers to better suit the preferences of their golden years. Maybe they will travel to other lands, like our older youth are encouraged to do, to bring back stories and souvenirs that will educate and entertain the rest of us. They might substitute physical labor for more intellectual endeavors, such as lecturing, writing, speaking, reporting on news in our neighborhoods, or coordinating social events. They could teach what they have learned over the decades, since enlightening the younger generations is a work of tremendous value, worthy of compensation. They may choose to volunteer in their community by watching young children, advising existing businesses, assisting in the libraries, overseeing group projects, visiting the sick, or comforting those more prone to being lonely. Such continued involvement in the lively activities of our city fends off depression, self-doubt, and an early demise. And if the benefactors of their service do not provide sufficient recompense to sustain them, then the priest certainly will, for these efforts all have merit.

"With broken hearts and contrite spirits, we pledge to take care of each other in Zion, a protection against the ills we might encounter. Nobody can predict what misfortunes may befall us. It is a purposeful mystery, like a veil over our eyes, to give us room to act, and we all risk defeat and discouragement as we take our chances at becoming joyful. Fate steps in to reward and to punish, for no reason other than to test our resolve. Sometimes crops fail despite planning and hard work, and there is nothing that can be done. Old age and sickness are part of our sojourn, reminders of our weakness and mortality. Wives become widows and children turn into orphans through no fault of their own. Individuals make mistakes, take a wrong path, and work their fingers bare without fruit to show for it. Catastrophe is an integral component of our journey, so we all must have a taste of it. Those who succeed today will fail tomorrow. We all take our turn, and there but for the grace of God we go.

"That is why the storehouse is so valuable. When calamity strikes, the disadvantaged are provided for out of the bounty of past donations, a portion of which is usually of their own making. As the priest in this area, they come to me with their claims and I, with my assistants and other advisors—as helpful—make sure they are supplied with all they lack. Most of the time, it is a simple grant of food, clothing, or tools—whatever is needed for the immediate future—and the recipients find their way back into prosperity largely on their own.

"For greater needs, we provide counsel in addition to the financial support, guiding men and women to profitable ventures, or brain-storming ideas on how to better control their expenditures. We offer opportunities for work that may have been hidden to them, or ask that they help on a community project in return for some of their support. In this way, nobody relies on the storehouse for their survival for too long. Yet while they do, they have the satisfaction of knowing they are still contributing to their fellow residents. Their self-respect and loving standing in the community are preserved."

Jubal continued to be surprised by the workings of this holy city, and was ready to rejoin the conversation, the demands of his private thoughts having been quenched.

"I recognize that food and wine get used up and cannot be returned, but what if someone in want received items from the storehouse—like a cloak, or shears for her sheep, or a table and cushions for her house—but then found her footing and no longer needed them. Does she return those objects to you?"

"Well, perhaps," speculated the stonemason. "The items would belong to her at that point, just like any other private property. She would be responsible for those goods, and hopefully she would do with them as she deemed appropriate. Nobody else would have claim on them, as she would be steward over the articles.

"If she had the wherewithal, she would have purchased or traded for them in the first place. But lacking the means, she may have borrowed the belongings for a short time from a neighbor, in which case she should definitely return them. Actually, we borrow things from each other quite often in Zion. Why purchase something that might be needed only once in a month or twice in a year? If one neighbor has the same object and is willing to lend to another, both are the richer for it. The first is spared the expense while still being able to do her work, and the second is pleased to have been of help. Wanting to stand blameless, the borrower would return the item in better condition than when it was loaned, maintaining and repairing it so that it can be shared by the next person. We all avoid waste by shunning unnecessary production, and thereby may devote our energies to more fruitful endeavors.

"However, back to your original question. Yes, if someone no longer needs an item and it can still benefit another, whether it be provided by our common supply or earned in the free marketplace, then it is given to the storehouse. But it could just as easily be given directly to someone else who would profit from it, saving them a trip to the priest. We all have each other's interests in mind, and look out for our wants.

"When a cloak is too worn to be of use, we sew the fabric into a coat or a veil or some other garment, or cut it down into cleaning rags. Very little is discarded. If in our evil natures we might be prone to waste the goods of another, we surely would not think to waste our own."

"Ours is a unique system of distributing wealth. It sounds efficient and fair, and there is nothing we have seen in our examination of the city to question its effectiveness," Mahijah complimented their instructor. "Is the storehouse able to handle the demands of our large and growing population, especially if it must sustain a weighty percentage of our residents?" The herdsman blushed at his words, having accidentally betrayed his inner longing. Joshua recognized the way the cloak maker had revealed his personal feelings, but gave it no heed in order to avoid additional embarrassment.

"Our numbers are mounting, to be sure, but the net increase has been consistently unhurried for hundreds of years, as our archives can attest. Due to our enterprise, only a minor fraction of our inhabitants ask for aid from our combined stores, and when they do, they seldom require more than temporary assistance. Virtually all of our disbursements are one-time or short-term.

"On exceptional occasions, when a person is wholly unable to take responsibility for herself, we provide for everything she needs without hesitation. But these cases are truly rare. Aging parents are cared for by their natural, capable children, or by volunteers akin those mentioned earlier. Family members tend to the perpetually sick, with cousins, aunts and uncles, and nearby residents pitching in to lighten the load. Orphans very quickly find new homes, taken in by adoptive parents who are willing to serve in perhaps the most noble of roles anyone can hold. Nobody is forgotten or left alone, for loving neighbors open their homes to any in emotional, spiritual, or temporal need. Many of our suffering people do not even cross my threshold, as they are supported by acquaintances without me being the wiser. It is our way, and we rejoice in it.

"Please recognize that, in their official capacity, our justices are not involved with the storehouse in any way. They contribute to it, and may receive from it, obviously," Joshua continued. "Nonetheless, it is not their place to control our private funds, whether they be consecrated for the general good or not. Government is force—a sword pure and simple—to be employed with great restraint and only in proper venues. Lamech must have explained that we do have occasional conflicts necessitating a magistrate, misunderstandings or remorseless offenses. But coercion has no place in our financial affairs. We must be free to work, free to give, and free to accept."

"With such a merit-based approach, do we not run the risk of creating envy between the more industrious of our residents and those who contribute less?" Jubal chose his words carefully, hoping to relieve his discomfort by exposing his own personal wish. He was still interested in the lesson, though the afternoon was starting to wane.

"Not really, not as long as we are all giving a full effort. You see, we are all equally rich, all financially alike. Our economic system eliminates all forms of perpetual poverty so that there are no poor among us. There are no separate classes based on wealth or profession, no special statuses as a result of notoriety or office, no ivory pedestals or towers to display fleshy idols. No person possesses that which is above another.

"We retain what we earn in proportion to our responsibilities and our just desires. If one father has five children, he must ensure that he can feed them all, and only donate to the storehouse what could be used to feed a sixth. Another father with but three young ones in his house will only keep enough resources to make those three comfortable. In this sense, everyone in both dwellings is well-fed, and any excess is bestowed for the benefit of some other family.

"The first father might need a larger residence than the latter, but they both have shelter sufficient for their needs. One person will want to learn music, while another pursues accuracy at the bow and arrow. A practiced archer might incur more expense than a flute player, but both are at liberty to pursue their individual activities and equally happy with their pursuits. It means little if one profession requires silver and the other copper, as they each have all that they could desire. It is perfect equality, unique as each person herself can be."

"What of those individuals who refuse to work, or prefer to seek bread handed to them by the roadside instead of eating it by the sweat of their brow? I have been constantly cautioned that we are free to choose, but is living in that manner an unacceptable choice?" Jubal knew the answer to his question, or at least thought he did, but he was now determined to be thorough in his investigation. His mind was set to join Zion, and he must not have reservations about his decision.

"Persuasion and long-suffering: these are the tools best suited to turning the idle from their bad habits. You are correct as always, dear artist.

Nobody can or should be forced from their languor, even if wasting time and capital in the midst of their own abundant earnings. Our people recognize a long-term avoidance of work and begging in public as being completely different from the borrowing of items we already discussed, or from receiving sporadic donations from neighbors. They are prepared to address this trouble with charity, by refusing to participate in transactions that add zero value, by discretely involving the priest, and by continuing their reliable contributions to the storehouse.

"This is the solution to helping those who start down the road to foolishness and sloth. Once the otherwise capable beggar in the street realizes that her actions will not be rewarded, that her unwillingness to make an effort is not a valid reason to receive payment, she will discontinue her unworthy actions. Gentle reminders of our unconditional, our unmistakable love for her, mild tokens of mutual promises made, and tender admonitions to participate with us once more are all that is needed to promptly halt the practice. When caring ministers plainly reveal the principles of Zion, the idle tend to recover from their dissatisfaction. And the priest stands ready to evaluate exceptional long-term needs and provide appropriate solutions until the person can stand on her feet again. We do not abandon anyone.

"However, it is possible that they will abandon us. Some have grown weary of our attempts to help. They will not come into our homes for meals and company. They refuse to educate themselves, to find new work, or to volunteer with upcoming projects. Eventually, they decide to leave Zion. At that point, their hearts have changed so much that they no longer feel a part of our society. Their attitudes become so different that they no longer wish to live among us, and choose to depart for other lands. It is a sad situation, but we cannot force them to stay, for doing so would not be loving.

"We can, on the other hand, supply provisions for their journey, then watch and pray for their potential return. Living apart, many who have left for other nations come to appreciate that they have made a mistake and wonder if they would be welcome again among us. Of course they would be! I have personally witnessed many such happy returns, including a reunion with one of my sons. After the sadness of her loss, great elation is felt at the reappearance of a prodigal."

That was not the answer Jubal had expected, but it satisfied him.

"As you remember," the flute player spoke as he tapped the middle of the bench, moving to one side so that the teacher could sit between his two pupils, "I was once rich, not as much as anyone in Zion, but enough to think myself special—superior to the poor who encircled me. I took pleasure in the notion that I could oblige people to do my bidding, either through the promise of gold or the threat of its power. I assume that there is no place for such feelings among this society, lacking as we do any poor to mistreat."

Joshua conceded the point without complaint, taking a seat as he said, "We have no poor in any sense of that word. There is nobody above or below another. Since we are all equal in the sight of God, we each desire to act towards our neighbors as he would. Goodwill permeates our streets and squares. We are rich in our relationships, overflowing in friendships, plentiful in talents and pastimes. We are as challenged as we wish to be, our curiosities never satiated, our peace never abated. As wealthy as you may have been in your past lives, neither of you have quenched your thirst in the wells of our abundance. I hope that someday soon you will."

The three men sat in silence, enjoying the last of the afternoon warmth and considering what lay before them. The musician and the shepherd were worn out. It had been a long day, full of instruction that stretched their minds and seared their souls. They were loath to abandon their seats, fearing that the magic of the day might break once they set foot back in the streets. The priest suspected what the two friends were experiencing, having entertained many past guests in a similar manner. He allowed some time to pass before rising from the bench.

"Will you join me for dinner?" Joshua asked both of them at once.

Mahijah rose and replied, "It would be our pleasure, but we cannot. Lamech and his loyal partner, Zillah, are expecting us at their house tonight, and promises must be kept. May we stop by to visit another time?"

"You can guess my response, dear brothers. You know where my house rests, and I am seldom far from it. I look forward to conversing with you again, perhaps just one at a time when next we meet. Say *hello* to Naamah for me. And Jubal, thank you for your gift. I will make sure it is put to good use." Joshua walked slowly back to his front door, turned to wave at his friends, and entered his habitation for the evening.

Jubal and Mahijah stood and started their journey back to the farmer's house, turning a corner and taking numerous paces to ponder the last of the instruction they had received before either of them spoke.

"How did he know of the silver?" Jubal asked the shepherd, already predicting the answer.

Mahijah shrugged, as unconcerned as he was unaware of how the old stonemason had divined the musician's donation to Zion's storehouse. It did not matter how he knew. The coins were in trusty hands. They would now benefit someone else as much as they would have helped Jubal.

The friends continued their walk in silence. The streets were as busy this night as they had been the first—more restrained than earlier in the day, but again brilliant with lanterns and torches in posts on the walls. Whatever was happening tonight, they were confident it would be as entertaining and productive as every other night they could imagine in this enchanted city.

They passed through the market square, also a much more subdued place than when they had encountered it earlier that very morning. All but the last of the vendors were packing up their stalls, though some performers looked as if they would remain a bit longer to amuse lingering friends. Children and adults still walked through the square, but not to purchase. It appeared that the forum was to serve as an extension of whatever activities were happening in the streets. The citizens of this city certainly made good use of their space.

Before long, the travelers approached Lamech's house. They had only conceded to ask directions twice, their comfort with the sociability and protection of the city giving them the nerve to impose. They were amazed each time not only at the willing helpfulness of a random passerby, but at her intimate knowledge of who Lamech was and where he kept residence. On reflection, they should have reacted differently. It should not have been a surprise that any arbitrary stranger in this slice of Zion would be cooperative, courteous, and an acquaintance of their farming friend.

With relative ease, the men arrived at the farmer's front door. Before announcing their presence, they paused to give each other knowing grins, noticing for the first time that there was no lock on the entrance to Lamech's house, but only a simple latch similar to that which they had seen on the storehouse doors. Their knocking was greeted with squeals of delight from inside. A gaggle of children burst out from behind the opening wood and under the threshold, hugging their recently-adopted uncles and insisting that they enter the house without delay.

Inside the familiar dwelling, the men found their room and beds just as they had left them, as if expecting their return. A bit weary from their tutoring, the uncles joined the family for dinner—a simple meal as sustaining and cheering as they had enjoyed the previous night.

In the middle of eating, Lamech's eldest child joined the banquet. Married and expecting his first child, he was his father's son, with black hair and a stocky build, though standing a little taller than his patriarch. There was unmistakable happiness on his face as he greeted the travelers.

"You must be my new uncles," he laughed, winning approval from his younger siblings as he extended his hand. "Please excuse my tardiness. My name is Cain. After spending the day harvesting dates with mother and father, I stopped off at my own house to reassure my wife that all was well. We are to have a baby any day now, and she is much more anxious about my whereabouts than ever before in our marriage. I cannot blame her! I will be your guide in the city tomorrow, and wanted to make your acquaintance before you retired for the evening. Have my parents been treating you well?"

"As well as two long lost uncles might expect." The shepherd considered himself fully assimilated into the family at this point. "We shall hold ourselves fortunate to be in your care tomorrow."

"Will you have enough time for a morning meal before we leave?"

the artist smiled as he took Cain's hand in turn.

"Yes, easily so, though I no longer rise as early as father. That is one aspect of being a farmer I do not miss. He will probably be in the fields again before I arrive to collect you. How much more harvesting do you have this week?" Cain looked to his father at the head of the table for a response.

"With your help, we made great progress today. I trust all of you are happy with your work," Lamech included his younger children in his praise, "for I know that I am. But we will need one more day, I think, and not a full one at that. I hope the rain will wait for us to finish. We should definitely have all the fruit gathered in before nightfall tomorrow."

"Good," Cain replied, turning to his uncles. "I will come by to fetch you after breakfast. Bring your walking sandals, for I have much to show you."

The expectant father embraced his mother, then all of his siblings. He gave a final goodbye to the whole room and left to comfort his spouse.

After dinner, the whole family was entertained, first by a poetry reading from one of the girls, then by a scary story from one of the boys—both original works. Lamech asked one of the children to read a short passage from Enoch's book, as the basis for an animated discussion. Zillah updated everyone on the impending birth of their first cousin and reviewed approaching activities and assignments for the house and the farm. The family then engaged in a brief discussion about local government actions, giving the younger children a chance to ask questions. Finally, each person was asked to think about any hardships that they could make lighter, such as a nearby family lacking food or clothing, a lonely friend, or a neighbor struggling with an emotional loss. The whole gathering was an uplifting experience.

The farmer explained that this was a regular event in the household, a chance for everyone to meet face to face for instruction and learning, renewing their common bonds and remembering how much they loved each other. The uncles could not have asked for a better ending to their most recent adventures. When the children were dismissed for bed, the cloak maker decided to retire at the same time, he being drained from another full day.

The musician rested on cushions at the far end of the main room near to the fire, his eyes bedazzled by its dancing flames. From their soft conversation in the middle of the chamber, he knew that the man and his wife were still awake. Eventually, they too rose from their seats and bade him a good night, heading off to sleep.

The ideas racing in his mind gradually slowed until there was but one thought remaining. If its inhabitants could accept him, he would be content to be the poorest man in Zion.

PRUDENT WELFARE ENRICHES ALL

8

Lie Down in Safety

JUBAL WAS READY—*MORE* THAN ready. With his promised escort soon to arrive at the front door, he was eager for a third day of touring Zion. Despite being the last to retire to bed the previous night, he had risen earlier than anyone else in the house. Anyone—to be exact—except for Lamech, the owner of the house and a farmer who was always the first to awaken. Jubal found Lamech already hard at work with some morning chores, his wife and children due to rise from slumber a little later to perform their own appointed tasks.

Jubal, the visiting flute player from Haner, decided to assist with the farmer's morning routine. It was comforting to some degree to contribute a bit of work to the household, in part as gratitude to the man and his wife for taking him and his traveling companion into their home and treating them as kin—despite an endless array of pre-existing children of their own. Donating his effort was heartening to a larger degree because, after only two days in the City of Holiness, the musician more fully recognized the innate human drive to work, to help out in some way, to labor for his own good and for the benefit of those around him. It was a belief he had witnessed in action as a guest in this house, along the streets of the city, and over the course of intense discussions. It was satisfying to put the principle into practice for himself.

Maybe he was being prodded in this manner by his conscience, that tiny voice we all have inside of us that nudges us this way or that, directing us in soft and subtle ways to do what we know we should. Perchance prodding was an accurate description of the feeling, but for Jubal it was more of a light that shone within him, illuminating his proper path in such an inviting way that he felt pulled instead of pushed towards it. And it was not pure emotion either, but a combination of feeling and thought, for his mind was lit up as much as his heart was brightened.

He knew that he was always free to decide his path, regardless of any shining or pushing that might be going on inside him. Personal liberty was the foundation of all choice. Depending on the inspiration he felt, the motivation to attain some desired goal, he could heed the prompting or not. It was peculiar for him to consider such a topic. He confessed to himself that his thoughts had been atypical, even odd, since arriving among this humble and industrious society on the first day of the week. His attitude and outlook were definitely changed as a result of his novel experiences, despite the brevity of his stay. His heart was different. He was a new man, and he liked his new self.

Standing in the residence mid-chore, adrift in contemplation, he abruptly realized that the fire now burning within him had been present from time to time since the days of his youth. He recognized fleeting instances of the same feelings from his past, such as while in the company of his attentive parents as they lived in their small house against the inside walls of the city of Haner. He remembered a similar feeling when deciding how to treat his two younger sisters, and when choosing whether to give a fallen coin in the marketplace back to its owner, or to keep it for himself. The light shone in him when he was deciding if he should play one last song on his pan flute, or return home for supper as promised. Those were good moments for him, happy times of intermittent joy.

But then he grew up. The slaughter of his parents and sisters, the loss of his wife—presumed dead—to the villainy of a conquering army, the enslavement of his fellow residents within the ancient city that was his home, all contributed to turning his heart cold. He appreciated that in reality it was *he* who chilled his *own* soul, who ignored the inner radiance until it was nearly extinguished. He further realized that the dimming of the light started well before the invasion of Haner and his subsequent descent into deep despair as a beggar in its byways.

Jubal stirred from his musings and finished helping the farmer with his chores. It was still quite early, but the rest of Lamech's household had risen and were completing their own tasks. Zillah, his wife, quietly gathered their children to leave for their agricultural labors of the day—harvesting their crop of sweet, juicy dates. The children whispered their goodbyes to the younger of their two uncles, gripping him in their traditional hugs of acceptance, and then the whole family was away to the fields.

Jubal shook his head in amazement at how merry the children could be so early in the morning, knowing they were skipping off to a full day of strenuous, back-breaking work in the hot sun. He loved their spirit, their vitality. He loved their seemingly endless optimism. He loved *them*.

The artist entered his borrowed bedroom and looked down at his friend and traveling companion, Mahijah, the shepherd of Haner. The old man was still sleeping. Jubal removed from his robe his flute, the one he had made famous as a musician of great talent in Haner's streets, and started to play a bright and cheery tune. The music from the custom-made pipes produced its desired effect, rousing the herdsman from his dreaming. Mahijah twisted a little on his bed of straw-filled linen, squinting his eyes to look at the source of the intruding music, then squeezing them tightly in an attempt to retreat back into slumber.

The artist chuckled at the sight: a grayed and world-worn man tossing about like a spoiled child. He persisted in blowing more of his tune through the flute until the shepherd stirred again. "Mahijah, it is time to wake," the musician whispered as he nudged his friend, continuing to harass him in a playful way until he finally gave in and sat up. "Our nieces and nephews have all left for the toil of their farm. They send you their love and well wishes. You should have seen their faces as they left, as happy and energetic as ever. But now, you have only me for your company until our guide arrives to show us the city. So up, arise old man. Get up! The day dawn has broken."

Mahijah stroked his gray beard with one hand, the other scratching his head as he dreamily replied, "I slept like one of the babes who claim us as their uncles. So, Cain has not yet arrived, is that it? Excellent! I would like a bite of breakfast before venturing out into the streets."

"You are in luck, sleepy one, but do not dawdle taking your bodily sustenance. Cain will assuredly be here very shortly to nourish our minds and souls. You remember our plan for today: he is to show us a little of his work on the streets and roads, and walk us through the city. We have seen but a limited portion of it as yet, though what we *have* witnessed has been most satisfying. I am pleased with the progress on our quest so far. We have learned much of the ways of Zion and how its inhabitants have achieved lasting happiness. But there is still much to see. Up with you!"

Jubal left the chamber, allowing his friend to gather his wits and to shortly join him in the main part of the house.

Mahijah sat on his soft and comfortable, borrowed bed. He gathered up the blanket that had kept him warm throughout the chilly night. He sighed with the contentment of a sailor safely come home from a long and hazardous voyage. He felt tranquil, serenely at ease. Like his artistic friend, he had learned much from the inhabitants of this strange and wondrous land, and was already determined to remain among them if he could. He wanted to join their purpose in serving each other, convinced he could still deliver value through his efforts in spite of his advanced years. He could thereby contribute to the common savings that kept Zion's residents secure from the whims of chance, the scourges of war, and the plagues of disease and drought.

He thought back on what had been his gloomier days, a life of struggle and despair, the rejection by the family of his childhood, the death of persons he loved, and the resulting loneliness. After surviving two famines, he left his native land of Sharon and journeyed to Haner, desperate to discover what little joy he could in raising sheep and creating quality cloaks from their wool. He found some pleasure in befriending Jubal, meeting him after the war with Heni's king ended five months earlier. The support of his younger associate gave Mahijah enough courage to listen to the wandering prophet, Enoch, the seer of Zion, and to survive their arduous trek of six days through the desert. With the extra strength his musical companion was able to impart, they both arrived among the occupants of Zion, despite the herdsman's weaker condition.

Awakened to the present once more, the cloak maker arranged his blanket neatly on his bed and prepared for a walking tour of their host city.

A firm rapping at the front door announced Lamech's oldest son, Cain, arriving as promised. He swung open the door without waiting for a response and walked into his father's house, making himself comfortable while his uncles—he had adopted the moniker his younger siblings used to identify the two visitors—made final preparations for their excursion. He was as happy and at ease now as when he had first introduced himself the previous night at dinner. He seemed the model of physical health and mental stability, jovial in his comportment while poised in his conversation, never presumptuous nor vain. Either of the uncles would have been proud to call him their son.

"How is your lovely bride?" Mahijah asked as he finished the fruit, bread, and water that served as his morning meal. He considered bringing something along for a mid-day snack, but decided not to worry about what he would eat later in the day. "And what of that baby soon-to-be? When do you expect her arrival?"

"They are both strong ... and impatient. The latter is eager to join us in the world, if her kicking be any indication, and the former is eager to be done with carrying the first. We think the baby will be a daughter. She is due in two weeks, though being our initial child we are told not to anticipate exact timing on the blessed event. My sweetheart is a little drowsy, as would be predicted, but I have energy for us both."

Cain was more talkative than his patriarch, and the uncles were glad to hear of his excitement. Mahijah had twice experienced the joy of parenthood and grinned in agreement at the zeal of the father-to-be. Jubal could only sympathize with the enthusiastic anticipation of receiving a child, though he thought it easy to imagine the thrill a newborn must bring.

"Excellent news," Jubal chimed in. "We must thank you in advance for agreeing to direct us today. Let us be on our way so that you may rejoin your wife before too long. We do not want her to think we are taking advantage of her husband's generosity. Though something tells me that a woman who would join herself to Lamech's household would not allow such thoughts to trouble her much."

The trio left the house. Cain was careful to close the door against any possible weather, and led his uncles towards the northern gate, the boundary his two guests had crossed earlier in the week in company with his father, mother, and siblings. As they walked, he began a history of the founding of their city, starting from when Enoch first received his calling by God to preach to the societies throughout the region in hopes of convincing them to pursue good and righteous principles.

That was over three hundred years ago, and their city had flourished since the beginning. Of course, its population was not always as numerous as it was currently. The city started out with only a small group of settlers: two families from Enoch's homeland where his fathers lived, and three others from outlying lands who were converted by his preaching. They bound themselves to each other, determined to protect their small town from every danger and, at the same time, to provide a prosperous and temperate environment in which to raise their children.

Little by little, bit by bit, they expanded from their humble origins into a larger city, until eventually they constructed the gates and towers, houses and forums, and public domes that lined the inner spaces of its walls. Their population growth was now overwhelmingly organic, though their evangelical work had not ceased. Enoch routinely raised up and trained a cadre of prophets to assist him with his preaching. They continued traveling throughout the wide world to this day, preaching the principles of Zion and hoping that their audiences would be convinced of their words and join them back in their happy nation.

There were recent discussions about founding a second city in pastures further south, within a half-day's journey of the current location, but that was still many years away. For those tentative plans to come to fruition, pioneers would be needed, volunteers to head south and settle the new city. They would surely not go unaided. From its storehouses, Zion would supply all that the adventurers could need to get started. From its strong men, labor would be forthcoming to build the first defenses and dwellings, and from its wise women, education and elegance would spring to fill their households with learning, laughter, and love.

From its populace, a leader would be selected to direct their efforts and to offer her name to the new habitation. What an opportunity it would be to settle a brave new city, brimming with the prospect of fresh exploits! The expectant father hoped to be a part of that eventual work, and was willing to take the reins of leadership, if his neighbors wished it of him.

"Do you see the lane here?" Cain asked, pointing with his whole hand towards the ground upon which the trio trod as they made their way to the northern entrance. The uncles responded in the affirmative, recognizing the mysterious coating on its surface from when they had first arrived in the land. The same covering, though more course, reinforced the road they had taken to approach the city.

"This is part of my stewardship. I was once part of the team that created this smooth mixture that makes rolling our wheeled carts so easy. You see, for the last many years it has been my task to maintain the streets of the city in the northern precinct. At first, the assignment by itself did not require enough work to keep me occupied, so I still farmed like my father, but on a much smaller tract of land. I was also able to help my family with their larger lands during peak sowing and harvesting seasons. During those times, I noticed that ruts and grooves were more prominent inside the gates, where there was much more traffic, than they were on the outside roads. I got to talking with some friends about how we could make the streets more durable, and we came up with a mixture superior to that which we had used in the past.

"Our innovated slurry took slightly different materials, much more time and effort to prepare, and more skill to properly apply, but it was obviously worth the extra expense. The street on which we now walk was the beginning of an experimental trial to gauge the mixture's potential success. Once we witnessed that it held up extremely well to heavier traffic, our quadrant of the city decided to cover all its internal avenues with the sludge. It was so popular that I started a new business, winning contracts to pave our portion of the city. Fortunately, there were a lot of friends from my childhood keen on helping me with the endeavor.

"Last spring, I leased out my farm so that I could focus exclusively on this new enterprise. If it continues to prosper, I might even sell my land, giving all attention to my roadwork, maintaining and repairing it as needed, and inventing better ways to aid travel. I could take the technology with me to the second city if asked.

"I do need to be prudent, however. There is already competition from a different improvement being rolled out in the eastern quadrant. It is a unique application using new paving material, golden in color, with future plans to extend it on the streets to the south and to the west before covering our northern lanes."

Cain was obviously very excited about his past and current successes, and about his future commercial potential, even in the face of what sounded like a strong rival technology.

"Your father must be very proud," offered the musician sincerely, understanding and appreciating the ideas being conveyed. He was reminded of the revolutionary pan flute of thirteen pipes he had witnessed in the bazaar just yesterday, a vast improvement over the flute of only nine pipes which he possessed. Novel creations and techniques must be an integral part of this society. There was much still to learn of this place.

"Well, he is, but he would prefer me to stick with growing crops. Is that not always the case? Fathers want their sons to follow in their footsteps. I get it. I can always return to agriculture if the demand for my road services dries up, but I prefer this line of work. I find it more challenging and rewarding. Besides, there will always be another farming family who could make use of my small parcel. We will guarantee that it is not left fallow."

Cain continued his animated commentaries until they reached the middle northern gate, with its unusual pearl-like center, its ornate carvings of a man and a woman fleeing away from a tree, and its odd metal supports with a silver hue. The travelers walked right up to the circular door and examined it again, this time more closely than when they had first walked by it with the lad's father at the beginning of the week. Observant soldiers on either side of the open arch smiled at the pilgrims, but made no hint of impeding their exploration. Cain recognized one of the sentries as a family friend and walked over to him to chat, leaving the pilgrims alone to appreciate the delicacy of the imposing ironworks. He rejoined his guests after a few minutes.

"Are the other entrances to the city always open like this one? The gate does not look like it has moved the span of a hand since we arrived two days ago. And what is this dull, silvery metal? Not copper, that is certain," Mahijah stated with an inquisitive air, intrigued by the uniqueness of construction he was noticing. While such structures were unremarkable in Haner and Sharon, the very gateways and boulevards of this urban center bore witness to the wealth and industry of its inhabitants.

Cain was quick to reply. "Now that you mention it, not once in my life have I seen the gates shut, at least not these three on the northern edge of the city. I frequent them the most, and cannot speak with equal authority on those facing east, south, and west. I am fairly certain that all twelve are constantly unlocked and swung wide open as this one is now. We might ask one of the watchmen on the towers—or better yet—a captain in one of the sentry houses, for a definitive answer.

"What I do know is that our men and women are free to leave at any time. Our gates are never closed to intimidate, or to trap a person against her will. As for the metal, it is a relatively new discovery, first forged and implemented before my time. Although it is not as decorative as silver or gold, nor as shiny as copper, it is much stronger, so the artisans do not need as much of it to hold up our great doors. Still, it does hint a little of silver when highly polished."

"But if the gates are always open, what security can they possibly provide?" the artist probed. "Is there nobody concerned that an enemy might sneak in and attack the people?" To Jubal, the memory of the invading army of Heni, terrorizing its victims, was recent enough to cause some alarm.

"I see your point," Cain conceded, sensitive to Jubal's pain but not at all upset. He thought for a moment. "I think you are correct. It could very well be that *nobody* is concerned. For some time, we have not been threatened with either invasion or war of any kind. From reading our annals, I know that in former generations we had to defend ourselves against attackers, and some veterans still speak with awe about those glory days. Back then, they felt no fear in the midst of battle, even though the size of our force was always dwarfed by the numberless concourses of the opposing enemy. Our civilian population was never very large compared to any other cities or nations, and it is still rather small. Regardless, we have no reason to worry about any army attacking us now. Zion is the safest place in all the wide world to lie your head."

Mahijah took over the questioning from his friend. "We have no cause to doubt your word, nephew." He smiled at his own use of the familial label, happy in comprehending that he was comfortable enough to apply it to the young man he barely knew. "You are evidently responsible and wise beyond your tender years. Please tell us how our city is so safe, that its occupants cannot be bothered to shut its doors at night."

"We are prepared," Cain said with a matter-of-fact tone.

The cloak maker looked at the musician, then back at their nephew. They waited, expecting more of an explanation, but Cain seemed content with his response. He started to move towards a sentry house to the east of the opening in front of them. Mahijah stopped him before he could go too far, asking, "Uh, forgive our confusion, but what does that mean?"

"You know ... *if ye are prepared, ye shall not fear*. Have you not heard the expression before?"

The inventor retraced three steps back towards his uncles standing by the open gate and clarified. "My mother taught it to me from a young age, and she continues to teach it to my brothers and sisters. Joyful confidence is our inheritance, and it will be the future legacy that we leave to our offspring. If we follow the principles taught to us by Enoch, we can cast all doubt and fear aside and walk confidently in the security of our

God. This is the most vital of our arrangements, for it prepares us for spiritual safety. This preparation gives us courage to face the world in spite of possible evils.

"When we are following the path to eternal shelter, we waste no worry on the uncertainties of tomorrow, but fully immerse ourselves in the purposes of today: our ministering, our occupations, our uplifting amusements, and the charitable relationships that give us joy. Freedom from fear is essential, for it empowers the vision that drives us towards enduring bliss, and the goals we set to attain it. These principles are so much more important to us than is our physical safety. In a comparable manner, did you not make preparations before traveling to our nation, and did they not set your mind at ease to some degree?"

"Well, yes, we did. In fact, it was the evangelist who taught us about Zion—who gave us doctrines to ponder that would fortify us along our way—who suggested such steps. He advised us to be wise in our pursuit, to delay starting our journey until we were rested and with stores and shelter in place to make the trip more likely to succeed," replied Mahijah, recalling the instructions Enoch had given him and Jubal that late afternoon on the hill outside of Haner, and the arrangements the two of them subsequently made for provisions and tents.

"And though you were equipped, did you not still risk your own corporal welfare by traveling to our borders? The expedition was surely arduous and fraught with perils, yet you attempted it anyway. Each of our lives is precious, for they are the medium through which we prove ourselves, and I am positive that you value yours as much as any other man. Would you not have been safer staying in Haner by a warm fire, under a solid roof, with the company of familiar faces to sustain you?"

"In a way, yes ... I suppose," Mahijah stumbled at first to respond. "But I begin to see your reasoning. Despite having a plan and securing some level of vigilance, our journey was still hazardous, no question. And knowing the probable jeopardy, we opted to undertake it anyway. Why did we embrace that course? Because the threat against our souls was ever more pressing than the menace to our poor physical frames. We wanted to enjoy lasting happiness, and for us it was not to be found in Haner. We were willing to risk our minor comforts, our relative good health, and our very lives on the treacherous and fatiguing footpath to see what Zion could offer. And now, here we are, perhaps the poorest men in Zion."

The pun in Mahijah's concluding sentence was not lost on their escort. Apparently, the seer Enoch had been the original author of this witty title, bestowing it on himself in a comical, self-deprecating way. It was a play on words, an expression of modest pleasure at being a part of their fertile community, for there were no poor in the city.

Cain gave the shepherd a knowing grin. "Yes, and here we are safe, though decidedly *not* poor. In our houses, we have shelter from the elements. In our garments, we have protection from the cold. We have the promise of potency in the grains and fruits that cover our tables, the results of our hard work. Through our diligence, we leave as little to chance as we can, resolved to follow the divine admonition to labor with our might. And when our houses burst with the magnificence of more children, we have the unexploited pastures and fields round about to feed us. The world has more to offer an honest worker than she could possibly use up.

"However, this is just the beginning of our reserves, for our diligence extends to our fellow residents. Did you not visit with Joshua the priest yesterday at the storehouse and witness the massive provisions we have saved against future calamity? If we were *forced* to rely on those goods, we could withstand many years of famine, drought, and siege. We reduce the risk from such possible events by spreading our surplus among ourselves. We are prepared."

Cain was his father's son, and he was only getting started.

"We are a peaceful and loving nation, our only thoughts towards occupants of other lands being those of friendship and compassion. We know they fight relentlessly among themselves, which is a disturbing thing for us to hear. We abhor the thought of war, and would never seek to start one—not under any condition I can envision. But if some foe did elect to attack us, would we still be secure from their hostility? Without a doubt, yes. Our walls are as high, thick, and strong as any in the region, and they encompass our city with neither fault nor break. Our gates, when closed and supported by towers and sentry houses, could not to be broken by any war machines we have encountered. We keep all our barriers in good repair in case they must be used in our defense, hoping that the days of peace will endure, but ready if they are shortened.

"And yet, this is not the end of our protection as a city. We have no standing army, but every man of a certain age is expected to serve as a volunteer in our common defense. They meet together once in a month to review protective plans, have their armor and weapons inspected, practice their assigned skills, and ensure fitness to fight. They have been known to use this time to reconnoiter the surrounding lands and to rehearse fighting techniques outside our entrances. We sometimes see them marching through the streets in drill, and they have occasionally put on shows for our residents. While our part-time soldiers still take their duties seriously, their monthly gatherings are more social events at this point, opportunities for the older among them to relive tales of past battles, sing old songs, discuss current events, and share a meal or two.

"The warriors provide their own swords, shields, helmets, bows with arrows, spears and similar weapons. When old-age or sickness renders them unable to actively participate in maneuvers, they keep their equipment at home, passing it along to their sons or storing it close at hand in case of some emergency. Older fighters, kept in reserve in this manner, comprise the bulk of our watchmen on the walls, maintaining a constant vigil day and night. As you can see, we keep attentive lookout from the watchtowers there and there, and man the guard houses at every gate."

Cain pointed up towards the tall structures flanking either side of the archway. When the uncles were finished glancing up and seeing the guards, he beckoned them to follow him to the sentry house that he had attempted to approach minutes earlier, before being delayed by Mahijah. He continued to speak as they covered the short distance, arriving to stand outside the small, rectangular house.

"Even if we were assailed, our stone battlements and trained sentinels are but a fraction of our protection, for our leader would call out the elements to fight on our behalf. Our greatest defense, first and our last, is God himself. Maybe you have heard the rumors regarding the power Enoch wields to overthrow mountains and to turn rivers out of their banks? They are not rumors, although it is not Enoch who is commanding the elements. God gives his trusted prophets supremacy over nature to keep us from harm in extreme cases and to fight our battles for us. What can an army of men do to counter a flood of water summoned to wash them away and drown them? Or what resistance can a mortal military present against an earthquake called to swallow them whole, or against tons of earth to bury and crush them? We show our obedience to and love for our God by being prepared, and then he takes over and saves us through his miracles. I am told that we did not need to triumph over our adversaries in this manner very often before every earthly army trembled at the thought of facing us in battle. The reputation of our heavenly strength and resolve—of God's unmatched supremacy—has spread across all lands, and no king dares to challenge it. They leave us in peace."

Cain tapped on the door of the sentry house and was immediately greeted by a bareheaded older gentleman wearing some kind of leather and metal breastplate, with a sword girded about his waist.

"Hello there, Cain. Good to see you again. How is your father? Are those dates of his as plump as ever?" spoke the good-natured warrior.

The captain stepped outside to shake hands with all three of his visitors and chatted briefly with them, like friends who had been absent each other's company for too long. He confirmed for the group that all the gates of Zion were continually left open, giving several reasons for the policy. Primary among them was so that any sincere visitor or fleeing refugee wanting to gain access to the city could pass through an official entrance at any moment, receiving directions or other assistance from the soldiers on duty at the time.

Cain thanked his military friend for his dedication, then led the uncles back towards the center of the city, inviting them to continue their discourse as they walked through the busy street.

"I think that soldier was older than me!" Mahijah declared with amazement. "Nonetheless, he was still able to bear the weight of his armor and handle a sword. I envy his enduring vigor. He must be one of the reserves you mentioned."

"Yes, he used to work with my great-grandfather, but has retired from his monthly service. He still volunteers at the gate, wanting to do his part. He tells me that old men do not sleep much anyway, so he does not mind the early and late hours."

"As ancient as he is, that old warrior acts younger than our shepherd friend," Jubal ribbed at Mahijah's expense. "You should have seen your older uncle asleep this morning well past the rooster's crow."

The shepherd whipped back his head with eyes and mouth wide open in feigned disgust, laughing sarcastically without slowing his stride. He knew Jubal too well to think there was any malice in his words, however, he had never known the artist to jest like this before. The elder uncle took it as a favorable sign.

Jubal returned to their conversation on the security of the city. "We can observe that Zion is safe from outside harms, but we have seen no soldiers on duty inside the city. Do we not have a force in place to keep harmony amongst ourselves?"

"We mostly keep in good graces with each other, as I am sure you have already noticed, with very little need for armed officials or soldiers roaming our streets. If there is a conflict, we almost always resolve it before it grows too severe, as fellow citizens amongst ourselves.

"If someone is accused of instigating an injury, but denies any wrongdoing and the matter cannot readily be settled, we form a small group for everyone's protection to escort her to a judge to be heard. The magistrate might ask for volunteers, paid or not, to provide temporary security during a prolonged hearing, but those situations are rare. Every once in a while, a cluster of families might hire a chaperone for a special event, or if some rowdy youths are causing problems, but then again they usually just get a volunteer selected from their own ranks to assist.

"We look out for each other, proactively lending help. If my wife and I are traveling away from our abode, we let our friends next door know of our planned absence, and ask that they keep an eye on the house and animals for us. Have you looked closely at the front door of my father's residence? There is no lock, no reason to barricade our houses even when we are away.

"Plus, if ever there *were* reason to need soldiers in the city, we already have a small army of them standing by. As you will remember, every man from young to old has weapons at the ready in his dwelling, for the protection of his own family and for Zion's larger defense. Force is available, but is seldom necessary."

"What about the force of law?" Jubal raised another topic that was sensitive to him. The flute player had once been at the mercy of an unfeeling king who had imprisoned him, albeit in luxury, over the course of the recent war with Heni. "What keeps us safe from an unjust judge?"

"My father told me how you had talked with him about our governors. The method of their elections and their inferior status to our voters are great hedges against the abuse of their authority. If the people determine a magistrate is being manipulative or exploiting her seat for personal gain, we can remove her by vote. We have very few laws, and if I am not deceived, their number has been steadily dwindling. A review of our formal archives, supported by the family histories like the one you studied in my father's house, can tell us for certain. We employ even fewer bureaucrats to twist or multiply these scant regulations to their selfish advantage. This leaves amazingly little actual power in their hands.

"In addition to their experience and wisdom, our judges are revered for their ability to detect truth from error, and to be both persuasive and firm. They rely on these talents—instead of on brute force—to administer justice, and on their deputies or the people to deliver and hold suspects when needed. All legal proceedings must be carried out in full public display while the light is shining, so that nothing is performed in secret. Judges must be present at punishments to certify that no excessive harm is inflicted.

"We respect the privacy and delicacies of our citizens, and all are treated equally and fairly before the law—at least such is our intent. Of course, we mutually pledge before God to act with integrity, respect, and honor regarding our fellow beings and concerning divine commandments, fully expecting our Creator to hold us accountable before him. Righteousness is our ultimate security. Through these practices, we are safeguarded from internal strife."

By now, the morning was better than halfway spent. The trio had been walking as they spoke, and were expecting to see more of the city, but a distinctive sound stopped Jubal in his tracks. It was the melody of a pan flute—but not any pan flute. This instrument emitted an unmistakable ring identical to that of the innovative device he and the shepherd had heard in the marketplace yesterday morning. Without a word, he swiftly crossed to the opposite side of the street towards a low house with three small windows and a roof that looked like pottery. His ear had not lost its skill, and he was sure the sound was coming from that building.

He arrived at the window closest to the front door and peered inside, Mahijah and Cain following close behind in his shadow, curious to see what had drawn his interest. A slender woman with gray hair was standing at the head of an attentive assembly, her wet lips moving effortlessly across the ends of the large pan pipe in her hands. Jubal recognized that flute, with its thirteen pipes and bronze supports, and was in awe at the coincidence. It was the same instrument he had borrowed from a young lady in the market just yesterday, the one she encouraged him to try for himself, for which effort he earned four pieces of silver from the generous crowd.

There was no mistaking the classroom setting. A dozen students, mostly children with some adolescents and adults sprinkled in, occupied chairs arranged in the shape of a horseshoe facing the instructor. Their youthful faces were rapt, their bodies were still, and they each held flutes of various shapes and sizes, quietly at rest in their laps. As the teacher finished her demonstration, she bowed courteously to the light applause of her pupils, then noticed the strangers at the window.

"Hello there," she called from the front of the room, her apprentices swiveling in their seats to follow her diverted focus. She realized that she may have startled the watching faces, still a little confused and unsure of how to react, which hesitated at her school window. "Would you like to come in and join us? We have plenty of room. Do not worry your heads about a single thing. We are all safe here."

PREPARATION
PROMOTES SECURITY

9

NO MORE STRANGERS

JUBAL WAS CAUTIOUS. HE DID not wish to intrude on the musical training taking place in the small house before him, but he desperately wanted to participate in it. From the front of the class, the slender woman who served as its teacher noticed the conflict in his eyes and slowly walked towards the door to let him and his two cohorts into the training room. She was an older woman to be sure, with gray hair and hints of wrinkles about her face, but carried herself like a maid of lesser years. Her polite students, twelve in number, remained seated while she walked past them and opened the door, inviting all three of the men standing in the street to enter and be a part of her instruction.

Jubal relaxed and walked through the threshold. He was still not accustomed to the kindness he was receiving in the ancient and formidable City of Zion. Since arriving three mornings ago with his friend, Mahijah, the shepherd and sewer of cloaks, he had been treated to a candid hospitality that he could never have expected. Farmers, stonemasons, inventors, and priests not only willingly welcomed him and his traveling partner, but also dedicated hours of their lives to educating them regarding the principles that made this land the most joyous in the world. Children instantly adopted them as surrogate uncles. Parents served them warm meals, provided them with comfortable beds, and trusted them with the safety of the most beloved in their household. Zion was not, as claimed by storytellers of distant lands, a horrible place full of heathens and criminals lustily seeking destruction and mayhem. Its residents were the exact opposite: industrious and free, purposeful and resolute in their desires to serve each other and their god. He truly had nothing to fear.

"Please come in and sit with us. We love to see our enrollment increase in size," the teacher entreated as she closed the door behind them. Three attentive children perceived what was happening and fetched chairs from a corner of the chamber, one for each of their guests. Others made space in their crescent-moon layout for the fresh arrivals, smoothly integrating them as they would any other newcomer to the class, receiving them with cheerful chatter.

Jubal, the flute player from Haner, found himself sitting between two young boys. Mahijah, once from the land of Sharon but more recently shepherding in Haner, sat across the classroom opposite from his friend, with a young girl on one side and a middle-aged man on the other. Their host for the day, the part-time farmer and full-time Zion enthusiast named Cain, was perched one seat over from Mahijah, with an adolescent girl to his side. The students were unperturbed by the interruption, evidently accustomed to guests joining them unannounced.

"Are you interested in the flute specifically?" the master instructor queried, returning to her place at the head of the class and looking directly at the guest musician who had entered her laboratory.

Jubal's hand instinctively reached for the custom-made pan flute that he kept in his robes. After giving away all his money yesterday, it was his only remaining possession—apart from the clothing that hid it—the one item from which he was unwilling to part. He loved his instrument, if ever a person was able to love an unfeeling object.

The touch of those beloved pipes reminded him of his past life, one that had ended nine days ago when he ventured from his homeland and sought the gates of this holy city. Formerly an affluent musician famous for his skill at producing melodies, he was at that time more married to his work and his malicious pride than to his actual wife, a sweetheart from his youth. He fell victim to pernicious passions and greedy warfare, and was on the brink of completely losing the will to live. Reduced to begging in the streets, penniless and destitute of the yearning to make music again, his heart was cold, and his soul hollow.

On the brink, but not in the drink.

Luckily for the musician, Mahijah had appeared in miraculous fashion to save him from his own despair not once, but twice. The first time was when he arrived in the flutist's land in the aftermath of a horrifying war with the king of Heni. The rival king deployed his army to attack the city of Haner, destroying much of its infrastructure and squeezing its surviving inhabitants under his malevolent thumb. The foreign regent demanded a duty of twenty percent of everything his new subjects possessed, allowing them to return to their broken houses and burned fields in exchange for the perpetual tribute. Fleeing an unrelated famine and the loss of his family in the land of Sharon, the shepherd occupied as his own an abandoned house in the countryside, started to raise sheep, and began selling in Haner's market square the cloth and cloaks he made from their wool. He befriended the musician during one of those trips, heartening him with his spark of optimism despite past troubles, and convincing him that all was not lost.

The second miraculous time was when he had convinced Jubal to join him in seeking happiness by listening to a seer named Enoch, come from afar with a message of hope and deliverance. Together, they sat on a small hill outside Haner, enthralled by the words of the preacher and instantly embracing his advice to travel to Zion and learn from its inhabitants. Now, they were beloved guests in that very City of Holiness and, for the moment, unwitting students of an expert flutist.

"Yes, he is," answered the young lady sitting next to Cain, across from Jubal and on his behalf. "He is a remarkable musician. He has played the very flute you hold in your hand, master. I loaned it to him yesterday in the marketplace so he could treat me to one of his songs. We should bid him play another for the whole class."

Everyone looked towards Jubal while he stared at the young lady, recognition slowly spreading over his face. Across the room, Mahijah was grinning from ear to ear, unable to restrain himself.

Cain chuckled out loud, smiling as he rubbed the black hair of his head, and said, "You are plainly feeling more at home than I had imagined, younger uncle. Yes, we must hear a tune from you without delay. And once I inform my parents of your rediscovered talent, they will be expecting another performance from you after we return from our tour of the city."

Cain was the eldest son of Lamech and Zillah, farmers living in the northern section of the city. His regular responsibility was to maintain the streets in this sector of the city, having invented and marketed a slurry to cover its avenues that made them more resistant to rain and smoother for traffic. Along with their many children, his parents had received Jubal and Mahijah into their home the morning of their arrival and kept them as guests. Despite sharing stories, meals, and warm fires, Jubal for some reason had not yet played his instrument for his hosts. He was not completely sure why, but would follow Cain's admonition and not withhold his music from them any longer.

The master walked towards Jubal with her hand extended, offering him the large flute so that he could play the group a song. He respectfully declined the instrument.

"Thank you, kind woman, but for my next piece," Jubal paused as he rose from his chair, turning again to look at the young lady and taking on a formal air for comedic effect, "which will be an admittedly *stunning* piece of musical artistry, I will rely upon my famous flute of nine pipes."

Bending at the waist, Jubal gave an exaggerated bow as he revealed his personal flute from behind his garment, holding it high above his lowered head in both hands. He looked ridiculous, and the students *loved* it. They all clapped and cheered as their teacher elegantly stole to the corner of her room to await the guest musician's piece. He recovered from his pose, then walked to the front of the room and turned to the master, mouthing a large *thank you* with his lips, causing her to curtsey in reply.

With a last scan of his classmates, and with an anxious breath, Jubal closed his eyes and began to play. It was as if he were a boy once more, floating through the streets of his childhood, playing the songs he had treasured for both their simple beauty and for their salutary effect on his patrons. He forgot about past pains, focusing only on present joys, and his audience floated along with him.

His song ended and he dropped his flute down to his side, opening his eyes. The room exploded with applause. All the students jumped up to congratulate him on his moving recital, the familiar young lady pressing forward to give him an unexpected hug. He was no more a stranger in this adopted land. He was home.

The master moved forward and congratulated her guest, thanking him for his recital and inviting him to remain as long as he liked. Jubal looked over to his two friends and decided that it would be better for them to continue their existing plans for the day.

As the trio expressed their gratitude and moved to leave the school, they could hear the trainer reconvene her tutoring. "Now class, let us take Master Jubal's performance under critique. What emotions did he successfully convey throughout his song? What techniques did he use to paint a picture with his notes? Did you notice how command of transitions and breath control extended certain themes? What benefit did his performance enjoy by being played on the smaller flute compared to this one? We will want to contrast ..."

Her voice receded as the friends departed the school and walked across the street, taking a seat on a bench by the far wall. They sat in silence, enjoying the fresh air and sunlight, pondering the concert they had just enjoyed. Regrettably, the artist's lingering grief had been so great that, after a good five months of friendship, this short exposition was the first time Mahijah enjoyed the privilege of hearing anything from Jubal's flute. Sensing a new aspect of his joy, he embraced his loyal companion in thanks for the music. It was worth the wait.

"You have talent, my friend," Cain commended the artist as he rested his hand on Jubal's knee, tapping twice before returning it to his own lap. "Your good company, my dear uncles, has already been ample compensation for my time as your attendant this day, but now I think I may have incurred a debt. I truly enjoyed your piece, Jubal."

Turning to Mahijah, he continued, "My older uncle, what singular skills must you be hiding, which could give advantage to us all?"

"Oh, my skills are worn and of little use, though my heart is willing, rest assured of that," replied the cloth weaver, who was happy to let his friend bask in the glory of his melody a little longer. "And yet, if ever there were a place for me to revive my talent and multiply it through assiduous exertion, Zion would be it. I think my hands and arms might even start to regain their strength if allowed to linger long enough in this land."

"Nonsense!" Jubal shouted indignantly, unwilling to permit their friend to belittle his own worth.

"Certainly!" Cain shouted simultaneously, confirming for their friend that his skill and stamina would blossom in this land of opportunity.

Jubal looked earnestly at the inventor and commenced complimenting his companion. "Mahijah makes some of the highest quality, stylish cloaks I have ever seen. His customers in Haner will tell you the same. They are not overly fancy, but sturdy and easily worn, beautiful in their simplicity—*elegant*, I would call them. He brought the last of them with us on our trip, packed on his mule, which is still sheltered in your father's barn. If I am to play for your parents tonight, I insist that he first display the excellence of his handiwork. His hands may be a little weary, but they have yet to sew their last stitch."

Cain looked in agreement at the musician, then faced the herdsman and started encouraging him, saying, "I have no doubt that your sewing prowess is already great, nor that you can find no better place than right here in Zion to enhance it."

Mahijah was grateful for the genuine support and compliments, but he was not satisfied to lounge in them for long. After a few minutes, he raised his head to the sky and asked, "How is it so natural for everyone here to accept us into their lives? Do not get me wrong, I long for such a rapport with my fellow beings. It is just foreign to me."

Jubal felt a swelling boldness in defending the principles of Zion, countering his friend's question with one of his own. Taking the preacher's role, he said, "Are *their* actions so alien, wise one, or are *we* the foreigners?

Just because we consider a custom, a tradition, or an outward attitude to be unusual or odd should not give us cause to reject it. Disparate actions are not automatically ill-advised, and less-popular paths are not necessarily dangerous. I confess that this new culture is strange, but purely because we are limited by our personal experiences. We think that the manner in which the nations of Haner and Heni treat each other and their respective subjects is typical, the only conventional approach. We have become so hardened by the emptiness of our past, by the cold that shrivels each chamber until they are too small for warmth, that we find it hard to envision anything else. But in the presence of this society's burning sympathy, our hearts are beginning to thaw—as least mine is—and we observe that the actions of our native peoples are no longer normal to us. What we have experienced, for barely three days in Zion, is solid and real for me, the way life should be. It is so thick with truth and compassion, so alluring, that I would pursue it at the risk of it being only half-true. Have we not found that which we have so earnestly sought?"

"Yes, I think we have," Mahijah reached out to take Jubal by the hand. For the first time since arriving in Zion, the friends openly expressed the measured opinion that they shared: Zion was everything Enoch had promised it would be.

Noticing their emotion, Cain took up the conversation, allowing them to recover and relax in quiet. "The acceptance you feel among us is real; it is genuine. We have learned that being altruistic mandates receiving individuals as infinitely worthwhile for their own sakes. It is part of eternal law. We love others simply because they exist, not due to any talent they might display for our entertainment, nor for some advantage we may gain through their association with us. We love each other as we love our God, as we love our very selves. This is the root of Enoch's teachings, that we display charity towards each other as our Creator has towards each of us.

"Charity can be difficult to express—sometimes, in verity, difficult to feel—surrounded by a population so at odds with each other. By design, we are unique, every one of us facing the blessings and challenges related to our personal variety. By contrast, our fallen and lustful state is uniform, as we are all similarly subject to our cruel and craven natures. But we are trying to treat everyone as God would want us to treat them, better than they might want or expect to be treated themselves. All are the same to us. Unconditional affection is the common impetus in all that we do."

"At our core we are the same, I can see that, but on the surface we can be so different. Does that not create conflict?" Jubal asked. He could tell that Cain was enjoying his role as guide and instructor.

"As humans, we certainly have common traits and desires, basic similarities that even the youngest of our children can identify. But even during your short stay, you must have noticed the diversity in our society. Male and female, short and tall, thick and thin. Our skin colors differ from the lightest to the darkest, a reflection of the various cultures and traditions from whence we spring. Our clothing, houses, hobbies, and occupations all mirror the personal preferences we develop over time. The distinct insights of each individual adds tremendous value as we progress. Why would such differences cause us distress? We *embrace* such variety. True diversity between our inhabitants is a happy byproduct of who we are, of our innate freedom to chart our futures. Every exceptional, distinctive, or odd person seeking to be happy is welcome to join with us and contribute.

"This is why Enoch suggested you come to our land in the first place. Our gates and arms are open to everyone. Zion must receive all who wish to accept our ways and join our ranks, else it ceases to exist. A significant number of our occupants were not born in our land, but immigrated from Heni, Haner, Sharon and other places. When we reject sincere outsiders because they are different from us, then we have rejected our God and his teachings, and cannot be justified.

"No matter her history, anyone who is willing to adopt our culture, learn and abide by our common commandments and principles, must be allowed entrance. Are not these values and ethics the very reason for foreigners risking refuge within our borders? Are these not the principles that drove both of you to seek us out? Our greatest strength is the shared dedication to righteousness that will lead to true happiness, denying none who come unto us in sincerity. Together, we can gain the precious pearl that eludes any who seek it alone.

"And upon joining our people, the aspiring foreigner becomes a part of us. She is one with our company. We make it our deliberate duty to assimilate those who add to our numbers. We cannot allow our brothers and sisters to feel from us any sense of being outcast. Starting with the priests and extending to the least among us, it is our pledge to gladly accept all whom we meet. We strive to be true friends to those around us, ever on the lookout for those who might be isolated or lonesome.

"In a practical sense, we cannot be close confidents with everyone. Time, energy, ignorance, and location are some of the limits that we must tolerate in this temporary world, overcoming them to the degree we are able. Still, we would require infinite lifetimes to become intimately familiar with all of our fellow sojourners. It is just not possible. So we do the best that we can, which is all that we can do. Not everyone can be our regular acquaintances, however we cannot in good conscience deny our goodwill from any brother who asks to be included in our lives. If we can offer only temporary companionship or relief, at least we can ensure that our brother connects with those who can serve him better.

"It befits us to engage an unfamiliar face whenever one is encountered, for once we meet a person and engage with her, hateful prejudice and odious envy immediately start to abate. The more we become acquainted with our fellow man, the more we build a hedge against falsehoods and cruelty towards her.

"You will agree that we cannot blithely declare to be welcoming and then not act accordingly. Words alone will not save us, nor give comfort to those who are lonely or ignored. The claims of our mouths and the intents of our hearts must be proven with our deeds. It is essential that we be vigilant in our empathy, ever rejecting hypocrisy and backbiting as quickly as we encounter it. In doing so, not only do we display true devotion, but we create emotional safety through love and respect."

Mahijah added an inquiry to the lecture. "But what if, despite all our efforts, someone is forgotten? Or what if, in a moment of weakness, we are purposefully mean-spirited towards our neighbors."

Cain sighed and said, "It does happen from time to time, but we are learning from our previous mistakes. When our minds are vigilant and our hearts attuned, heaven compensates for our weaknesses and follies. We apologize and make concerted efforts to include all who wish to be involved. For example, the city is designed to have all our residents live within its boundaries. In addition to the security this arrangement provides, it guarantees a physical closeness that stimulates becoming more intimately aware of each other, and reduces the probability that someone will be inadvertently overlooked. Structure constrains outcomes, and proximity encourages awareness. In this way, we see and are seen by those in our neighborhoods, making it so much more difficult to carelessly forget the admonition to be our brother's keeper.

"We organize ourselves in small communities within the city for the same reasons. Local teachers, assistants to the priests, keep formal watch over our numbers, careful that none are lost. But if a sheep strays or is accidentally cut off from the flock, we seek her out without delay or spared expense. As a shepherd, you must have worked the rescue of many a precious lamb. What exertion of body, heart, or mind would you have neglected—what corner would you have left unsearched, or how many would you have left for a wee while on their own—to reclaim her back into the fold?"

Mahijah thought back to his past herds, remembering how important each sheep had been to him. He nodded understanding to their mentor for the day. There was almost nothing he would have avoided to recover one lost member from his own flock. If love in some form could push him to suffer stiff hunger, cold rain, and rocky terrain to recover one of his precious lambs, how much more would he be willing to endure to save a brother?

"Of course, the Physician prescribes repentance in large doses, as well as ample and regular courses of forgiveness. We regularly fall short of our ideal selves, a function of our mortal shells. Exhausted bodies, heavy hearts, distracted minds, and wounded feelings all contribute to innocent errors, slothful inattention, deliberate nastiness, and vile sin. All of our inadequacies have been anticipated and will amount to nothing but sounding brass and tinkling cymbals, as long as we remain firm in our commitment to confess our faults, recompense those we have wronged, improve our ways, and walk with charity."

Cain stood to continue their stroll, then realized his belly was complaining for attention. "I fear that my sermon has gone longer than the congregation can stomach, and that my stomach has been neglected longer than it can tolerate. Shall we find some relief in the marketplace? There is always some flavorsome thing to fill us up, even at this late hour. Moreover, the spices brought from foreign lands by our adoptive citizens can be a real treat."

Jubal remained seated, looking up at the street master, insisting that he respond to a final question before lunch. "You, your family, Joshua the priest—everyone we have encountered—have displayed such benevolence towards Mahijah and me to almost make us blush. We recognize that we are strangers, and do not deserve such thoughtfulness. But are we much different from other visitors who have traveled to this land? Would you treat anyone else as well as you have us?"

Mahijah shifted uncomfortably on the bench, sensing a touch of contention in the question, though consoled by an equivalent surety that the maintainer of streets would return a constructive answer. The uncles were mildly startled to detect, for the first time, a touch of frustration in Cain's voice.

"Do you not believe your own eyes, your own hearts? Do you not believe me? You both know the answer to this question, uncle. Everyone is respected here. There is no legitimate fear of being ridiculed or shamed. We appreciate everyone for who they are as a person. But beyond that, we acknowledge everyone for the person they may become. Why is it, do you imagine, that education and work and liberty are so prized in Zion? It is because we all seek to become our most excellent selves. In gathering together, we grasp our best opportunity for such success. The spiritual and emotional encouragement, the financial and physical support that a community of like-minded men and women can offer, virtually guarantees it. We partake in altruistic devotion to the God who makes it all possible.

"All are welcome—but none are constrained—to live in our city. If a person does not wish to adhere to our principles—the philosophies and practices that make living among us so appealing to her in the first place—she need not enter, or may leave at her leisure. Strangers who receive our friendship accept the foundations of our loving bond and are strangers no more."

Jubal brusquely took to his feet and started walking at a sharp pace.

"I am convinced!" he called over his shoulder jubilantly, leaving his old friend and new nephew to make an effort at catching up. His soul was afire and his eyes were awash. There was nothing more for him to ask or to hear on the matter. He was no longer a stranger in this land, but a friend, an uncle, a brother—a disciple.

"Let us get some of that lunch of which you spoke. But I must warn you," he continued, slowing his stride a little to allow his companions to rejoin him, then turning about to wink at the cloak maker and to flash a huge smile at the inventor, "I gave all my money to Joshua yesterday, and I suspect Mahijah to be equally poor. You may have to practice some of that charity you have been preaching. I am pretty confident your unfortunate fate today has been to entertain the poorest men in Zion."

The cloak maker shrugged with an elated grin as Cain laughed at his uncles. The inventor was undeterred, conceding, "Well, part of becoming a better man is helping others receive that which they lack, but that is a topic to be addressed on a full stomach. Of course you should know by now that the heft of your purse means nothing within these walls. I am sure we will manage."

Jubal had no doubt.

ADVOCATES WELCOME

THE ASPIRING

10

TEACH ALL NATIONS

JUBAL WAS CONTENT AS HE lounged on a bench by the far wall of the open market square, the receding desert sun bathing his face and arms in a golden warmth. The meats, breads, and exotic fruits sold by the vendors in the bazaar had more than satisfied the emptiness of his belly, quelling his transient discomfort. He was confident that hunger would not bother him again until well past the setting of the sun, much later in the day.

With care worthy of an old friend, he held in his hand close to his breast the timeworn pan flute that once provided him and his audiences countless hours of pleasing music. Since his childhood in the house of his carpenter father, he had played a myriad of songs from those nine pipes, carefully fashioned from strong reeds growing near the walls of Haner where he had lived.

His other hand rested on the shoulder of his traveling companion and dear friend, Mahijah, the shepherd and cloak maker of Haner. He was the same man who had planted a seed of hope in his mind and given him an appetite for seeking happiness by traversing the age-worn footpaths that crossed their desert lands. Mahijah felt old, wearied by a life of sadness and loss, but pleased now to join the musician in his sunny repose.

Their newest friend Cain, designer and maintainer of the streets they were frequenting, reclined on the same bench in half-slumber, unprepared for the combined attack of a morning full of walking and a stomach full of tasty treats. He had willingly—eagerly—agreed to leave his expectant wife and unborn child safely at their home to serve as guide and teacher for the day to his guests as they toured this unusual land and interacted with its occupants. Securely and mildly enveloping them, the revered City of Zion revealed its prosperity and cheer. As if wrapped within the folds of a cozy blanket, the companions each considered themselves fortunate to be enclosed in its affirming love.

Mahijah welcomed his friend's hand on his shoulder, reaching up to tap it with one of his own. He scanned the activity in the plaza before him. Individuals and couples, families and peer groups wandered through the colorful marketplace that was a preferred place for both business and social gatherings. The immense space was simultaneously bustling with movement and emanating an orderly calm. The herdsman marveled at the diversity in form and function that played before him. Shapes, sizes, and sounds of every sort reached his senses, from the odd accents of the men speaking in a corner, to the erratic blasts of practicing trumpeters against the far wall. Despite the farmers, merchants, performers, shoppers, and casual observers who teemed throughout the squared aisles that gave the area structure, there were no shouts of alarm or concern for mischief. Children played innocently, some underneath their mothers' cloaks, some amongst themselves at the edges of the square, and others circulating throughout the crowd. It was a happy scene. He sighed and closed his eyes, as content as his young friend.

"Cain, my young genius, have you drifted off over there?" Mahijah teased the dark-haired young man, son of Lamech, the farmer who had originally welcomed the travelers when they arrived in Zion three days ago. *Could it really have been a mere three days?* During that short span, he had progressed so much in his understanding and appreciation for this venerable city and its inhabitants. It felt like a lifetime.

It *was* a lifetime.

"Nearly, I fear, older uncle," the entrepreneur replied, making use of his now favorite moniker for the tall and grayed man whom his family had adopted as their own. Cain's innovative discovery from years ago had been used to pave the streets they walked that morning, and specifically the lane in which they were relaxing. "Jubal is so quiet, I think he is the one who has succumbed."

"You mean to say *younger uncle*, do you not?" the musician was glad for his unearned title. He truly felt a part of Lamech's adored ensemble, like family even to the young man before him who had moved away from his parent's home, albeit not too far away. "I would not mind spending the rest of the afternoon right here. I have never witnessed elsewhere such a display of genuine bliss as I now do inside these walls. We owe Enoch a debt of gratitude for sending us to you."

Enoch, the seer of Zion and wandering evangelist to foreign nations, had encountered the two uncles while he was preaching in Haner, the flute player's native land and the assumed one of the cloak maker, he being a refugee from the land of Sharon. The prophet taught them principles of happiness, the word of admonition received from God himself that Enoch had been commanded to share with surrounding societies. In their heads and in their hearts, the uncles recognized the truth of Enoch's words, and heeded his counsel to travel through the desert to experience Zion for themselves.

Scarcely more than a week later, they arrived in the suburbs of the land, meeting Lamech as he toiled on his farmland. They voluntarily worked side by side in his fields and were welcomed into his household as family. The next day, they were carefully educated in the financial customs of this people by Joshua, a former stonemason turned local priest and now keeper of the storehouse of God. The silver and gold deposited in that warehouse was greater than anything the two visitors could have together contemplated, but no greater than the accompanying principles of hard work and balanced welfare revealed unto them. Each day, they devoted hours to learning from their hosts about the spiritual and economic underpinnings that steered their neighbors towards lasting happiness. They were grateful for another day of revelation.

"There are no debts in Zion, as you know full well," Cain retorted, enjoying the effortlessness which the three men felt among themselves.

"Regardless of how inviting and accepting it has been, previous visitors have not always stood at ease within the very divergent culture they found in our land, at least not as quickly as you two have. Change, though hard, is the only way to achieve our vision of a better life."

"Of course, we are all aware that the two of you remain visitors in name only. I have seen the spark of comprehension and longing in your eyes, and witnessed your acceptance of the truths you have heard. As far as Enoch is concerned, when he learns that you actually made the journey he suggested and dedicated your time with us, he will feel amply compensated for his efforts. Actually, you just might see him at the end of the month when he returns from his travels, if you choose to follow your hearts and reside with us."

Mahijah had sensed a portion of the unending joy that comes from living as a disciple in Zion, and fully expected to remain in the city as Cain implied, though he had not yet vocalized his resolve. He knew that Jubal felt the same delight, for he had expressed as much to the old man, but a lingering reservation made the herdsman question if his young friend would also choose to stay.

"It is doubtless a difficult labor for Enoch and the other prophets, traveling as they do to far-off places to teach others about this one. How do they keep up their enthusiasm for the work while in the midst of so much sorrow and anger?"

Cain sat up to better focus on his response. "I can only imagine, as I have not made such an excursion for myself. What adventures they must encounter! But from what we have heard of their discourses here in the city, the source of their buoyant passion is plain: the worth of a soul is great in the eyes of God. That is any soul and all souls. He cares not only for those persons who listen to and obey him, but also for those who are lost, confused, or unaware—even for men and women who are vicious and mean, or who openly reject his love.

"The evangelists try to follow his divine example and do as their Maker would do. They cannot be justified in remaining in security while so many others suffer in ignorance or rebellion. They want their fellows to participate with us, to partake of the heavenly gift. Part of becoming pure in heart is helping others receive that which they lack. We spread the good news so that others will put it to the test, discover the truth of it for themselves, and join with us. It is simple charity."

"Then their work must be unsatisfying to them, even frustrating," the artist sighed. "When we went to listen to Enoch on the hill outside of Haner that sunny afternoon nine days past, thousands of its occupants had hiked to the outskirts of the city to hear him. We personally saw hundreds of its inhabitants walking away from his teachings and back down the mount. At least dozens were actively fighting against him, ever while he meekly endured. Before he departed to spread the word elsewhere, only the two of us were paying any attention. Two hearers among thousands is not much fruit."

"No. In spite of sincere efforts to persuade them, there are not many who accept the invitation, but do not think the missionaries disheartened. The preachers realize that some people hear the call without responding immediately. Those unwilling to follow in full may still pursue in part. They may take what principles ring true in their current condition and do the best they can to make those philosophies work in their own lands. A little at a time, hearers of the word see the validity of our values and implement them for themselves, reaching out to family and friends who are open to a greater bliss. They become doers of the word as they gradually adopt practices for living more fully.

"It is as if the preachers are cultivators, preparing the soil and sowing seeds as my father does in his meadows. They put their shoulders to the plow, patiently hoping that forthcoming partners in the work will be able to nurture the tender seeds they plant. Seeds grow into shoots, shoots produce luscious fruit ready for reaping, and future farmers of Zion—with their arms at the scythe—bring the fruit home. So our ministers teach and instruct as many listeners as will consent to their sermons, from the pauper in her squalor to the prince in his palace. This is why we actively—consciously—seek out those who might want to join us. Otherwise, we are not worthy of our condition. Zion cannot exist unless we give everyone an opportunity to be a part of it.

"By making such exertions for the benefit of interim outsiders, our prophets illustrate the absolute necessity of practicing their beliefs. This work is part of our purpose, our mission to find lasting happiness through noble objectives. We are willing to sacrifice the production of monetary riches, the comforts of home, and the days of our lives—tolerate chidings and mockery—in order to serve unacquainted foreigners. It is not enough to sit back and wait for others to come to us, but we must hunt them out among the leprous and the lame, the disgraced and the outcast, the haughty and the mighty in their own minds. We thusly sanctify our own souls, and cover a multitude of sins.

"And when our success is such that there is no more room within this specific patch of ground," Cain emphasized his point by raising his foot and stomping it on the dusty ground, "why, then we will settle new colonies in all directions of the compass, like stakes of a tent, duplicating the practices found in the center place.

"However, preaching the doctrines of our God is not the only means to serving others. The cultural, academic, and commercial fruits of the righteous walk we try to undertake are often more appealing to the residents of faraway lands. Sometimes, the only way alien kings and leaders, or their subjects, will allow our emissaries to assist them is by satisfying more tangible needs. They are not quite ready to follow our behavioral example, nor the practical yet spiritual advice we provide, but they are willing to receive of our silver and gold. So we accommodate them as much as we can without making their situations worse.

"We frequently send the bounty of our storehouses to feed those suffering from famine or drought. Far away victims of pestilence or injury receive adept medical care at the hands of our schooled physicians and surgeons. We provide expert counsel across virtually all subjects in which our skilled workers are trained, to include fishing, engineering, reading and writing, construction, sanitation, and farming. Though outright donations are common, we prefer to help the folks in adjoining societies develop their own worthwhile abilities, learn to care for themselves.

TEACH ALL NATIONS

"With due respect towards sovereigns, we send diplomats to urge peace among rival nations, attempting to appease all spirits of spiteful contention. We honor the rule of legitimate monarchs and avoid becoming entangled in their affairs. Wise words and the civic aid we can provide are often enough to prevent violent exchanges, but unfortunately, not always.

"When mischief arises and our would-be friends suffer, we can still deliver relief. We open our doors to those who flee before the armies of an oppressor, offering sanctuary until the threat is past. Alongside survivors of war, our builders cut and smooth lumber, chisel and lift stone to reconstruct their cities. We try to be generous towards the people outside our walls while ever protecting the people inside them. Recipients of this type of aid might stay with us for a short time, then go back to their previous homes. We will not violate their liberty. They are free to leave at any time, but if they stay, it is because they wish to live as we do and become one with us."

"Does the cause of Zion never sleep?" The gray-haired shepherd asked rhetorically, amazed almost to the point of becoming exasperated, as if the deeds of this people were too imposing for him to attempt participation in them. "Her citizens must lead lives of overflowing."

"I know, right? Is it not *the best thing* you have ever experienced?" expelled the young inventor excitedly, completely missing the point of his older uncle's comment. "There is always someone to help out, always an occasion to wake up and do something more, if one is of such a mind. It is part of our duty to teach others what we have learned, and to make them the subject of our love. We cannot be happy knowing that we might have helped others but missed the opportunity. And yet, just as rest from our labors is required, personal choice is paramount. Neither coercion, nor force, nor debasing ridicule should ever find a place amidst our influential tools. Liberty is a principle which we must respect, even if there are some who abuse it with tyrannical choices."

Jubal rose from the bench to reach his full height, his arms outstretched, his mouth opened in a wide yawn. The inventor took the gesture as an indication that his listeners were ready to end their tour for the day. He decided to conclude his discourse.

"Of course, our work takes many shapes—equally valid—based on our penchants and talents, and there is no shame in a suitable break from those duties. Today, mine has been to show you a portion of our city and to expound on some of its principles. I sense that our late lunch and most recent conversation will bring those obligations to a close. Will you stay the night under my parents' roof once more?"

The uncles were spent. True, their path around the city had not been lengthy, but the instruction from their guide exercised their minds more than they were accustomed, and they were ready to make an end of it for the day.

"We are thankful to you, Cain," spoke the shepherd from his sleepy seat, overwhelmed with his thoughts and feelings as he remained settled on the bench. "You, your generous father and thoughtful mother, your patient priest, and our devoted seer who started us on our path have each bestowed invaluable insight for us to contemplate. We cannot express how fruitful our conversations have been."

"Such is our most earnest pleasure. Our days have been more delightful with you to share in them," Cain responded in sincerity. He reached down to touch each of his uncles with a hand, pausing to let the reciprocal appreciation hang in the air a few seconds more. "Now, shall I guide you back to their house?"

The musician was inclined to meditate a little longer in the lane, and suspected his friend would prefer the same. "We can find our way, I think," he said, catching an agreeing nod from the older man with the corner of his eye. "Count on us returning to them later in the day, after we have had a chance to contemplate your lessons."

Cain smiled, then turned without another word and walked off towards his welcoming home and his awaiting sweetheart who helped to make it so.

The travelers were left to themselves. They sat in silence, sensing no rush to leave their bench. They sat some more, the inspiration of the last three days flowing within them like water from a refreshing spring.

They persisted in sitting.

Finally, they relented and stood, starting to walk. They wandered together through the streets in no particular direction, without a word to break the silence. At last, Mahijah voiced his complicated thoughts in the simplest of statements.

"I will stay here."

Jubal knew exactly what his old friend meant. He had anticipated the declaration, having the very same desire, but was apprehensive about being the first to vocalize it. Nothing could be the same for either of them now, the cosmos of their souls having been turned upside down. They were both categorically convinced that Zion would be their new home. Its spirit permeated every fiber of their beings, and they were converted to its philosophies. It was time to act.

All of a sudden, the flute player halted in his steps and wept. Great sobs—uncontrollable sobs—shook his frame to such a degree that he had to lean, nearly falling, onto the herdsman for support. The friends stood in the middle of the avenue, motionless except for Jubal's heaving sighs, forming shadowy outlines in the dying light. Time slowed for a span, then gradually regained its proper momentum.

Before long, Jubal gathered himself and wiped his eyes. "I would stay with you. I would commit to it this *very* moment. But there is something I must do before I can rest my head with ease in Zion. I wish to have nothing but a clear conscience from this second henceforth. I must return to the outside world—to Haner and to Heni—and recover my dear wife, if there remains in her a single breath to be saved. Tonight, we shelter once more with Lamech, but in the morning I must leave you. If God be willing, I will be absent only for a short season. But if God demands it of me, I will never return."

Mahijah understood, for he had heard the sad tale from the mouth of his once-troubled friend on several occasions, though Jubal never spoke her name to him. Unlike his deceased parents and sisters, his wife's body had never been recovered in the wake of Heni's invading army. The rush of its assault allowed little time to verify rumors that she was taken captive.

With no trace to be found of her in or around their demolished dwelling, the musician dolefully surmised that she was lost forever.

The shepherd recognized that if there were merely a *chance* that Jubal's spouse had somehow survived and was yet alive, his friend would have to seek her liberation. Despite the grave danger, he could not do differently, not after finding and embracing the source of happiness, the balm to heal his every hurt—as well as her every wound. He *needed* to rescue his precious helpmeet if her soul yet strove among men, or accept his own death as fair price for the attempt.

The uncles turned about and marched with great strides—grander resolve—to the dwelling of their adopted family. Cries of gladness and childlike hugs greeted them at the front door. Dinner at the farmer's homestead had already ended, but no matter. They were full from their much delayed midday meal and too eager to share the company of their brothers and sisters to worry about food. Understanding that his guests were returning that evening, Lamech had decided to skip one of his favorite activities, the neighborhood game night, and remain at his residence to keep them company. They asked the family to join them in the main room for a presentation.

As promised, the cloak maker retrieved his inventory of cloth and robes from the barn where his mule was resting, gaily presenting the particulars of his cloak-making craft found resident in his creations. They were impressed with the quality and care evident in the goods. He made a gift of the fabric to Zillah, and of the cloaks to Lamech and his sons, promising future alterations. He would *not* be refused.

Fixed on keeping his portion of their vow, the musician in turn pulled out his pan flute of nine pipes and described how his father had carved it for him so many years ago. Everyone was eager to hold the custom creation, and to admire its refinements. Jubal related as much of his musical background as he thought appropriate, then stood by the fireplace to one end of the low table in the center of the room and placed his instrument to his lips. From his childhood repertoire, he played one of his favorite tunes, and then another before his emotions ran too high to continue. The children danced about the chamber in gleeful response to his masterful music.

The uncles then sat down on plush cushions and unveiled to the household their plans for the future. The farmer and his family were elated at Mahijah's news. They would start helping him right away with finding a house of his own—they insisted it be located nearby—procuring new robes with sashes and sandals to match, and deciding on an occupation that would suit his situation. Zillah suggested that he concentrate on sewing cloaks and leave the more strenuous work of raising and shearing sheep to his future suppliers.

His transition would start in the morning with a visit to Joshua, the priest, to express his wish to join the community and to set a date for his welcoming ceremony, the occasion on which he would dedicate himself to the cause of Zion. That special event would be scheduled at a sufficiently future time to have all of his questions answered and to give him ample opportunity to absorb the ideals of his new people at a leisurely pace. Final integration as a new brother would be formalized at a second ritual, after another watchful interval to ensure his continuing commitment.

The household was equally enthusiastic at Jubal's announcement, though admittedly saddened that he would be leaving for a short while before officially joining them in the prescribed manner. Though he would not accept their offers of help, they showered him with hopes for a successful search and a speedy return to their home in the happy company of his treasured wife. They could not wait to meet her, and to hear him play his flute for them once more. In the morning, he would take Mahijah's mule and reverse his journey through Zion's northern gate.

The family delayed retiring to bed as long as they could, but before long the uncles found themselves alone in the main room. Only they two fully grasped the true peril that Jubal risked by his daring gambit, his proposed effort to pry his wife from the hands of her Heni oppressors. How could it be done? What chance did he have? The friends moved quietly to the barn, allowing their preparations for Jubal's imminent departure to mask the fear that turned in their stomachs.

Once finished, they crept back to their borrowed room, unwilling to disturb the members of their adopted family who were already sleeping. They both lay prone on their respective piles of finely cut straw, neatly wrapped in clean linen. Their eyes, unwilling to close just yet, gazed at the tiled roof. Neither would their ears relax, giving attentive heed to every whispered sound as if awaiting a thief in the night.

Please, God, let me save my wife was Jubal's only thought.

Please, God, keep safe my friend was Mahijah's only notion.

Ultimately their senses surrendered, and their bygone souls were immersed—tomblike—in that cyclic death from which we always expect to awaken reborn, refreshed and renewed.

At the close of the third day, the sun rose.

And so the friends parted—the rescuer to find his disappeared wife, and the cloak maker to commence his new life. Over the next six weeks, Mahijah received assistance in establishing a blueprint for his future in Zion, and began turning that plan into a blessed reality. His hours were full of activity and amity, the most busy, productive, and pleasing of his long existence. His body grew stronger with each passing day, and his heart emerged more humble, forgiving, and benevolent than ever. He was happy and fulfilled beyond his wildest aspirations. Love flooded his soul.

And yet, he allowed his mind to be distracted from time to time, remembering his musical friend and contemplating an imminent, triumphant return. It was not hard to do, for in his hands was a souvenir left behind by that young artist, a message as clear as it was prized. Jubal had entrusted his beloved flute into Mahijah's care, to preserve it as either a heartening token of their upcoming, glorious reunion, or as a motivating memorial to his tragic, selfless demise.

Life in Zion carried on, the mundane and the exceptional both serving to advance its residents towards their aims. At her poetry recital, Lamech's young daughter painted—with her words—striking, moving images, invoking occasional tears. Cain's newborn child arrived in good health—a girl, as expected—invoking a steady stream of joyful cries.

A neighborhood celebration followed Mahijah's welcoming ceremony, marked by heartfelt speeches, spirited dancing, and flavorsome sweets—including luscious dates from Zillah's pantry. To commemorate the event, young Naamah had sketched for him a drawing that was sure to adorn his future abode, an image of a huge flock of sheep being watched over by their shepherd.

Crops grew and were harvested, merchandise was assembled and sold, and streets in the northern sector of the city sporadically cracked and were repaired. Apprentice flutists were applauded at their concerts, and aged soldiers kept watch at their posts.

The end of the month came and went. It was odd that Enoch had delayed his homecoming, though not especially so. A seer must follow any impromptu inspiration he might receive, regardless of how it may interfere with his schedule. He would turn up when he was ready, when God's purposes for him were wholly ended. There was no call for concern.

Then one morning, it happened.

The cloak maker was sitting at his stool, his back to the sun, working a needle and thread through fine fabric to form the first of his newly-designed robes. He heard footsteps approach from behind him and then stop, but he was so focused on his sewing that he declined to be bothered by some passing distraction. He preserved his focus until an impression struck him concurrently in his head and in his chest with such weight that it could not be ignored. He turned and squinted, the sun in his eyes, barely able to make out three human figures standing before him.

He dropped his needle in the sand under the stool and involuntarily stood, shading his eyes to see more clearly. To his amazement, he perceived on his left hand Enoch, the seer of Zion, and on his right hand Jubal, his dear friend. Between them stood an anonymous, slender figure, leaning on the musician, long black hair enfolding a rejuvenated—almost glowing—oval face.

"Hello, Mahijah," spoke Jubal in a quivering voice. "This is Hannah, my much-loved wife. Do you happen to have my old flute lying about? I will need it when we visit Joshua at the storehouse. You see, we wish to join you and our people in being the poorest couple in Zion."

OUTREACH EXPANDS INFLUENCE

~ ~ ~

AND THUS WE SEE THE whole of the matter. Lasting happiness is our deepest desire, but can only be achieved while we are free to choose good over evil. When we are united with cherished partners through hard work and service, we become secure in our identities and esteem others for who they are, urging them to participate with us in worthwhile development.

The answer to sadness is more influence and acceptance, more preparation and charity, more equality and industry. To respond to sorrow, we require more noble action directed towards a unifying purpose, and more liberty to chart our shared course. For lasting happiness is a choice, and freedom is its bulwark.

As these values become fused to our very essence, then will we see as we are seen and love as we are loved. Then will we clearly realize that the poorest man in Zion is wealthy beyond the richest man in Babylon.

An Historical Sketch of Zion

WITHIN THE ANNALS OF HISTORY there is perhaps no city more feared and beloved than that of the legendary Zion. It was the original city of righteousness, founded by the prophet Enoch and his spiritual adherents around the beginning of the third millennium B.C. as a place of prosperity and refuge, located in the geographic area that would become known by some as Canaan, and by others as Israel.

For its enemies, it was a terrible place, a mighty city with troops so powerful and a leader so fierce that they could not be defeated in battle. Their prince would but speak a word and the earth would shake, great earthquakes opening in the ground to swallow entire advancing armies or their fortified capitals. With another utterance, the mountains would shift at their very roots and move to block invaders, or fall upon and bury them under their untold weight of stone and dirt. Rivers obeyed his command, turning out of their courses to drown aggressors, flood their lands, and wash away their crops. The very lions of the forest seemed to be under his direction, threatening to tear attackers apart as they marched against his people. Against such a force of nature there could be no victory.

However, there *could* be peace. For within the walls and lands of Zion, there lived and labored a gentle and loving people, striving for harmony amongst themselves and goodwill towards all nations. They were free, at liberty to associate as they wished, to work and recreate as they chose, to think and speak and worship according to the dictates of their own conscience[1]. Seeking lasting happiness was their mutual vision, achieved through individual goals and shared values.

They encouraged all forms of honest toil: farming, trading, skilled crafts, artistry, philosophy, and the like. They practiced charity and acceptance towards all peoples, sharing with needy neighbors in and out of their city gates—including foreigners wishing to unite with them—the great wealth they created through industry and innovation.

Their streets were full of animated discussions, friendly greetings, and laughing children, and were protected by high walls, determined defenders, stockpiled resources, and an enduring trust in God. But the welcoming gates of that glorious city were ever open, encouraging incoming visitors to join its ranks, and outgoing evangelists to proclaim the invitation. The light of the sun seemed to shine from within its borders, like a candle in the darkness, for above all else this was a place of righteousness. Its residents were pure in heart, and they walked with God.

As ominous and wonderful as Zion was, very little is known of its multiple-century history. Extant authored accounts are few and almost entirely from religious sources. The Bible barely mentions the city or its leader in either of the testaments.[2] An apocryphal Jewish text[3] is dedicated almost entirely to visions and teachings instead of contemporary historical events. Perhaps more historic details are provided by Mormon records, the most extensive spreading to 137 verses in one book[4], but its content is again—in the main—religious instruction and prophesy. References throughout another Mormon work[5] refer more to a nineteenth century implementation of the city than to the age-old one. Old Testament

---

[1] Articles of Faith, *The Pearl of Great Price*, The Church of Jesus Christ of Latter-day Saints.
[2] *The Holy Bible King James Version*. See Genesis 5 and Luke 3:37 as examples.
[3] *Book of Enoch*. See https://en.wikipedia.org/wiki/Book_of_Enoch.
[4] Moses 6 – 7, *The Pearl of Great Price*, The Church of Jesus Christ of Latter-day Saints.
[5] *The Doctrine and Covenants*, The Church of Jesus Christ of Latter-day Saints.

descriptions[6] of a City of Zion give the most meticulous portrayals, however they seem to be referencing a future occurrence of it. Nonetheless, some speculate that this anticipated instance will be modeled after the original.

If the written record of Zion is sparse, the non-literary, physical record is fundamentally absent. There rests no known solid remains of the city—no internal archives, no pottery, no tools, no burial mounds nor monuments, not even stony foundations to give an outline of where the city might have been located. One penned account[7] explains that this is chiefly because Zion vanished, that it was miraculously taken up whole out of the ground, rising into heaven along with its inhabitants. Compounding the evidentiary dilemma is the establishment of the city prior to Noah's worldwide flood, which would have undoubtedly complicated the topographical record and likely the geological one as well.

Of course, if the inscribed story and the ensuing flood are accurate, then one would not expect to find any physical remnants from the city itself. Future construction atop its vacated location, as suggested below, would effectively obfuscate discovering any chance, lingering confirmations in the future. While it is possible that artifacts from the city's inhabitants could have been transmitted to other civilizations, no such concrete remains of the city have so far been presented. Still, there is an encouraging, logical consistency in claiming that Zion disappeared without a trace, and then being unable to find any tangible signs of it.

Does the scarcity of traditional evidence mean that Zion was not? Some will contend this to be the case, citing the lack of archeological proof and scant reliable documents. Others will keep trust in the indirect witness of the written word, realizing that even historians and scientists live largely by theory, unable to personally verify every jot and tittle of human understanding. They gather tidbits of data, interpret and infer and extrapolate from second-hand sources, and do the best they can to recreate

---

[6] Ezekiel 40 – 42 and Revelation 21, *The Holy Bible King James Version*.
[7] Moses 7:69, *The Pearl of Great Price*, The Church of Jesus Christ of Latter-day Saints.

the past. Faith—trust in the experiences of fellow investigators—must inform their own research as well. For the purposes herein, reliance on the surviving archives will suffice.

The story of Zion begins with its mortal founder, a young lad named Enoch. This male name is of Hebrew origin, meaning *to train up* or *to dedicate*.[8] The son of Jared, he was the seventh generation from the first man, and great-grandfather to the Noah of flood fame. He was not to be confused with his cousin four times removed, a son of Cain by the same name who coincidentally also built a city that became self-titled.[9]

Enoch was brought up in the spiritual tradition of his forefathers, inheriting his perception of the divine from ancestors all the way back through Seth and Adam. He was raised to follow the commandments of God as he lived in the land of Cainan, among a people who tried to be righteous. He was accustomed to traveling about in the earth—locally to be sure—but also amid the neighboring tribes of distant relatives who had broken away from his parents and established their own cities and lands.

Enoch was still comparatively young in 3133 B.C.[10] when, at the age of 65 years, he fathered the Methuselah who would famously live to be the oldest chronicled person. At some point after the arrival of this most recent child, Enoch was in the midst of one of his travels when he was called by God to prophesy to those people living apart from himself, specifically to the inhabitants of Sharon, Omner, Heni, Shem, Haner, Hanannihah, and of the land founded by his distant cousin called by the same name. Among those detached relatives, warfare, murder, greed, and deceit were so common that even brothers of the same household would betray each other in pursuit of power, money, and fame. Having

---

[8] James Strong, *The Exhaustive Concordance of the Bible* (a.k.a. *Strong's Concordance*). See https://biblehub.com/hebrew/2596.htm.
[9] Genesis 4:17, *The Holy Bible King James Version*.
[10] The author relies on a purposefully simplistic approach to the ages of the Biblical patriarchs, anchoring the birth of Adam at 4000 B.C., and accepting the genealogies of the Old Testament at face value. Relevant dates sufficient for this work are thereby calculated, and arguments for or against the most accurate ancient calendar are decisively avoided.

abandoned the precepts of mercy and justice from generations past, Enoch had been sent to call them to repentance.

Despite the encouragement he assuredly received from speaking with his Creator, this assignment must have been intimidating for the relatively fresh Enoch. His proportional inexperience probably led him to think that he was not the best person for the job, or that people would ignore him because he did not know much. His hesitance extended beyond the nervousness of youth, for he did not consider himself a fantastic orator, being slow of speech. Perhaps in his mind the greatest obstacle to fulfilling his mission was that he was not very popular, thinking that everyone hated him.

There exists no explicit explanation as to why Enoch thought that all people, everywhere, disliked him. Perhaps it was hyperbole born of bitterness, but it would certainly not be a helpful starting point for someone bound to garner greater hostility as a result of his preaching.

But preach he did, receiving comfort from his God as he called upon the residents beyond his borders to wallow no more in their selfish and cruel activities, but rather to remember their Maker and return to the holy precepts taught by their ancestors. Purposefully avoiding the land of Canaan, he chose to expound his message from the hills and high places, and many people came to hear his story. The great majority of his listeners doubted Enoch's sermons, returning to their houses either angry or fearful, or at least unconvinced by the wild man who had come among them. Some few believed, and followed his counsel in seeking for themselves a path towards joy.

Over the course of time, adherents of the seer assembled together to build the City of Enoch, with its namesake as one of their most prominent leaders. It was here among like-minded brothers and sisters in the City of Holiness that they could fully attain the enduring happiness which the ministry of Enoch had promised. They were likely accompanied by families from his native land as well, others seeking the same bliss.

United in their desire to live uprightly, Enoch's people must have farmed their lands and raised all manner of livestock, constructed private homes and public edifices, and fashioned works of stone, wood, clay, and metal. They likely traded with each other in the streets and marketplaces, their hard work generating riches beyond description. They probably enjoyed private and public expressions of sculpture, music, poetry, paintings, theater, and dance. Their wide avenues were inclined to be full of laughter, conversation, and pleasing voices, and in their forums they undoubtedly engaged in all manner of dialogue and debate.

Their new residence grew to be a city of some size as a steady—if slender—stream of fresh disciples responded to their evangelizing efforts. Eventually, walls rose to enclose its center, but the gates of their glorious city were ever open, and a celestial light blazed forth for the world to see. For ultimately, God walked among them. They were a people honest and fair, free and welcoming, possessing hearts made pure through taking regular and consistent action upon their desires to serve.

Geographic references strongly suggest that the City of Zion was originally located on the eastern shores of the Mediterranean Sea, in the area that would later be claimed by the children of Israel. Along with the peoples revealed above, Enoch makes specific mention of the ancient land and people of Canaan. He also states that he stood on the mount Simeon, possibly a mountain by the same name found in the northern extremities of the area to this day.[11]

The name *Zion* is found frequently in the Biblical record, referring generally to God's people or to the land that they would inhabit. Over the course of time, the name became equivalent with the entire city of Jerusalem, though it began more specifically as Mount Zion, the Jebusite stronghold[12] on the lower eastern hill that was conquered by King David around 1000 B.C and subsequently used as his castle. Abraham had travelled that way not a millennium earlier, binding his son, Isaac, on

---

[11] Mount Simeon in the northwestern extremities of modern Syria, near the city of Aleppo. See https://en.wikipedia.org/wiki/Mount_Simeon.
[12] Mount Zion, the City of David, in southern and lower Jerusalem. See 2 Samuel 5:7, *The Holy Bible King James Version*. See also http://www.israel-a-history-of.com/map-of-jerusalem.html.

Mount Moriah, where the future temple mount of the capital city would be located. Previously and in the same area, he had freed his nephew, Lot, from the tyranny of local rulers, paying offerings to Melchizedek, the King of Salem and a near descendent of Noah, from the spoils of that battle.

With the old city of Jerusalem and its enveloping lands holding such significance in later generations, it is reasonable that the naissance of its influence could have blossomed from the days of Enoch, from the very spot of his habitation. The City of Zion was probably founded *exactly* here, establishing the future tradition of a spiritual center place.

Zion prospered in this sacred site for centuries. Enoch, and unquestionably others like him, continued their missionary labors, pleading with those they encountered to turn away from their misery and to associate with the people of God in gladness. Their joy matured line upon line as they learned to improve their condition through energetic purpose. The power and prestige of this city never waned as its population gradually increased, at last testing the limits of its walls. On the contrary, it is reasonable to conclude that Zion's glory continued to grow and expand year upon year, enduring 365 of such periods in total until about 2948 B.C.,[13] just prior to the birth of Noah. It stood as an example to the world surrounding it, shining on its hill for all to witness, matchless in financial and emotional wealth. Even the riches and fame of the future Babylon,[14] though doubtless noteworthy at its peak, would not approach the abundance and grandeur of Zion.

Then abruptly, the City of Enoch was gone. In an instant, the entire city, along with its inhabitants, was inexplicably removed—wholly intact—from the spot they had once occupied. No enemy had breached its walls. No pestilence had wiped out its population. No disaster had struck its fields and meadows. Yet the saying went abroad that Zion had

---

[13] Section 107:49, *The Doctrine and Covenants*, The Church of Jesus Christ of Latter-day Saints.
[14] Babylon's earliest founding dates to circa 2300 B.C., already 600 years after the removal of the City of Zion. Babylon achieved prominence as the capital of its empire between 1800 and 600 B.C. See https://en.wikipedia.org/wiki/Babylon.

fled. It had steadily thrived in every imaginable, virtuous way until it exceeded the bounds of its worldly enclosure and was suddenly taken up into heaven, to reside in the bosom of God.

Though Zion be fled, its history has not yet come full circle. Ever since the city's translation, the idea of Zion as an earthly utopia has inspired groups of people across the globe to strive for similar principles of lasting happiness in contemporary iterations. Philosophers have drafted dissertations regarding paradises improbable and lost, hoped for though rarely realized. Dreamers have composed melodies about living in harmony, imagining a world in which there would be no poor, and all could live as one. They parallel the faith and testimony of prophets who have proclaimed that a New Jerusalem, Zion's sister city, must one day be established. Only during brief intervals and in limited locations have certain associations achieved fragments of this ambitious ideal. The allures of a united community full of joy and prosperity are easy to understand, just as evident as are the wretched obstacles that oppose it.

And still, the dual promise is made that the venerable City of Holiness, now hidden, will someday be revealed for all to see as it descends with its inhabitants from above. Then will it be partnered with its modern companion—a second Zion—as it rises with its residents from below. Historians at that time will be quickened with ample evidence of glories long past to fill their chronicles, and copious declarations of present wonders to fill their reports.

As they do, the same wise values that once governed the City of Holiness in days gone by will continue to guide those who wish to make the majesty of a renewed Zion their everlasting home:

Happiness is our deepest desire,

Freedom empowers choice,

AN HISTORICAL SKETCH OF ZION

Mutual vision unites people,
Promising goals drive action,
Mighty labor yields abundance,
Surplus creates shared savings,
Prudent welfare enriches all,
Preparation promotes security,
Advocates welcome the aspiring,
Outreach expands influence.

The Author and His Book

DAVID BENSON, LEADERSHIP COACH, IS passionate about guiding business and community leaders to achieve their full potential. His business interests include leadership excellence, management integrity, motivating presentations, strategic planning, quality communication, unselfish employee engagement, and executive coaching. As a trainer and facilitator, he prefers an interactive approach to speaking that energizes audiences and challenges them to make immediate and significant improvements to their professional and personal lives.

David has over 25 years of experience in management consulting, corporate training, business analysis, and project management in a variety of fast-paced settings, from innovative start-up companies to industry powerhouses. The former Managing Director for Dale Carnegie Training of Utah, he was responsible for marketing, selling, and delivering content for professional development seminars and time-phased courses across the state. He has served as a consultant, presenter, and coach in the technology industry, advising over 100 small, large, and non-profit organizations at all supervisory levels.

In early 2019, David published a series of cohesive essays on establishing a transcendent, thriving society rooted in principles of freedom, unity, virtue, diligence, charity, and continual improvement. These precepts were illustrated through parables with a uniting narrative

THE AUTHOR AND HIS BOOK

set in and around the ancient City of Zion, an idealistic model of happiness, fulfillment, security, and wealth. Along with an historical sketch of the city, he gathered these stories into a single volume under the title *The Poorest Man in Zion*. His hope is that these essays will one day become familiar to millions, and that the book itself will become an inspirational classic in its own right.

Based on publications by the same name, David delivers ongoing *Leadership Excellence Seminar* and *Course* events across the United States. These in-person, full-day or time-phased trainings focus on the six key characteristics of dynamic, engaging leaders that comprise his Leadership Excellence Model.

In addition to dozens of technical certifications, David holds earned degrees in business (MBA, entrepreneurship specialization) from Utah State University, and in psychology (BS) from Brigham Young University. He is a veteran of the U.S. Army National Guard.

Raised in urban Virginia, he now resides in northern Utah with his wife and three of his six children. He enjoys kayaking, musical performance, and playing late-night family board games. His present, peculiar challenge is preparing for an Olympic-distance triathlon. Please visit www.DavidBenson.us for background and offering information.

www.ingramcontent.com/pod-product-compliance
Lightning Source LLC
Chambersburg PA
CBHW052026070526
44584CB00016B/1919